Hawks in Flight

Hawks in Flight

The Flight Identification
of North American
Migrant Raptors

PETE DUNNE
DAVID SIBLEY
CLAY SUTTON

Illustrated by David Sibley

Houghton Mifflin Company

Boston

ALL RIGHTS RESERVED
For information about permission to reproduce selections
from this book, write to Permissions, Houghton Mifflin
Company, 2 Park Street, Boston, Massachusetts 02108.

Library of Congress Cataloging in Publication Data
Dunne, Pete. date.
   Hawks in flight / Pete Dunne, David Sibley,
      and Clay Sutton. p.   cm.
   Bibliography: p.
   Includes index.
   ISBN 0-395-42388-0
   ISBN 0-395-51022-8 (pbk.)
   1. Birds of prey — North America —
Identification.   2. Birds — Identification.
3. Birds — North America — Identification.
I. Sibley, David.   II. Sutton, Clay, date.
III. Title.
QL696.F3D86   1988   87-18929
598'.91097 — dc19   CIP

Printed in the United States of America

KPT 13 12 11 10 9 8 7 6

Book design by David Ford

This book is dedicated to the memory
of Maurice Broun,
Hawk Mountain's first curator,
and to those who remember him.

Head-on Profiles of Selected Species

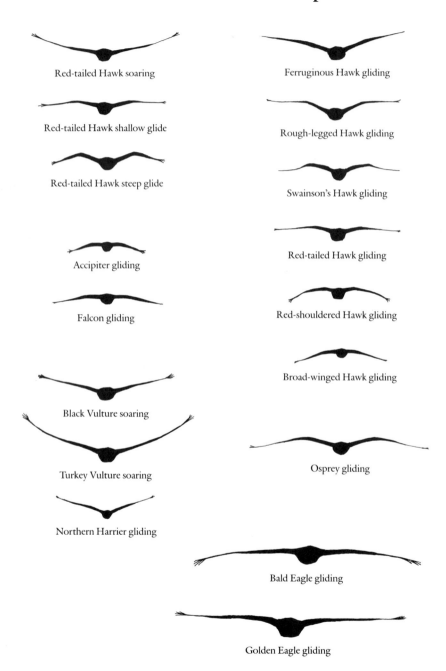

Red-tailed Hawk soaring

Red-tailed Hawk shallow glide

Red-tailed Hawk steep glide

Accipiter gliding

Falcon gliding

Black Vulture soaring

Turkey Vulture soaring

Northern Harrier gliding

Ferruginous Hawk gliding

Rough-legged Hawk gliding

Swainson's Hawk gliding

Red-tailed Hawk gliding

Red-shouldered Hawk gliding

Broad-winged Hawk gliding

Osprey gliding

Bald Eagle gliding

Golden Eagle gliding

Contents

Contents

Contents

Topography of a Raptor

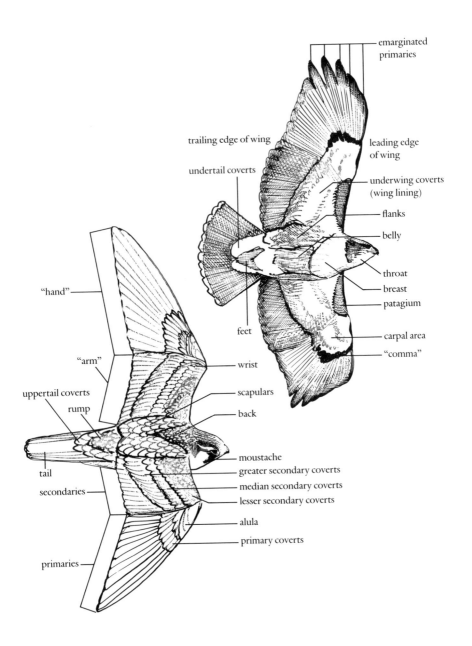

emarginated primaries

trailing edge of wing

leading edge of wing

undertail coverts

underwing coverts (wing lining)

flanks

belly

throat

breast

patagium

carpal area

"comma"

feet

"hand"

wrist

"arm"

scapulars

uppertail coverts

back

rump

moustache

greater secondary coverts

tail

median secondary coverts

secondaries

lesser secondary coverts

alula

primary coverts

primaries

Foreword

by Roger Tory Peterson

From March through May, and especially from August into the short days of December, thousands of birders and other observers clamber onto ridge tops or position themselves on lake shores and coastal concentration points to witness a ritual pageant — the migration of North America's raptors. At Hawk Mountain, Pennsylvania; Cape May, New Jersey; Mt. Tom, Massachusetts; Point Pelee, Ontario; Duluth, Minnesota; San Francisco, California; the Goshute Mountains in Utah; Derby Hill, New York; Charleston, South Carolina; and a thousand other locations, hawk watchers test the limits of their identification skills.

My first field guide saw the light of day in 1934, the very year that Hawk Mountain Sanctuary became a reality. In that rather modest first edition with the green binding, I portrayed the flight patterns of hawks as they appear overhead, the first time this had ever been attempted, except for a single black-and-white plate by John B. May in Volume II of Forbush's *Birds of Massachusetts.* That classic work was published in 1927.

The original concept embodied in the *Field Guides* — often referred to as the "Peterson System" — was to simplify, to make things easier for the tyro. The illustrations, whether they depicted birds perched or flying overhead, were deliberately schematic, emphasizing shape, pattern, and special "field marks." Prior to this, bird identification focused on fine points of plumage — on the characteristics of individual feathers or of eye color. To see these subtle characteristics, the bird had to be in the hand. The tool of the ornithologist was the shotgun.

In the half century since the first publication of *A Field Guide to the Birds,* the popularity of bird observation has grown exponentially and field identification skills have grown in measure. The scope of bird observation has grown so large, in fact, that it has become quite specialized. Different schools of birding utilize different techniques.

One, whose origin is rooted in the sophistication of modern optics (such as high-powered spotting scopes) is the school of looking close — the micro school of birding. Identifications of very similar birds are made by looking at the patterns of individual feathers (not unlike the bird-in-the-hand method used by the old shotgun school).

The opposite school is the school of looking far — sometimes called the holistic, or gestalt, school. Identifications of distant or fast-moving birds are made on the basis of overt shape, size, plumage, actions — the overall impression. *Hawks in Flight* belongs to this school. It is the direct descendant of the Peterson System in that it teaches identification by looking for field marks that are visible at a distance.

The authors of this long-overdue guide are eminently suited to the task. Pete Dunne, David Sibley, and Clay Sutton have invested nearly twenty thousand hours in the study of hawks in flight.

Pete Dunne, a familiar name to North American birders, was the director of the Cape May Bird Observatory from 1978 to 1987, and is now the director of Natural History Information for the New Jersey Audubon Society.

David Sibley, an artist and leader of international tours for WINGS, is one of the most perceptive field birders in North America. His drawings are graphic replications of what hawk watchers truly see in the field. His sense of flight and shape are unparalleled.

Clay Sutton, a photographer and environmental consultant living in Cape May has been among those most instrumental in the preservation of habitat in this key migration junction.

Acknowledgments

By conservative estimate, the thoughts, suggestions, articles, or spoken words of several hundred thousand individuals have shaped the text of this book and its illustrations. Budgetary constraints being what they are, we have been won over by the very convincing arguments put forth by our editor and have included herein only those names whose omission would constitute an indiscretion beyond all bearing. We thank Harold Axtell, Pete Bacinski, Seth Benz, Rick Blom, Pete Both, Jim Brett, Bill Clark, Harry Darrow, Bob Dittrick, Jim Dowdell, Howard Drinkwater, Greg Hanisek, Mike Heller, Paul Kerlinger, Harry LeGrand, Arnie Moorhouse, Frank Nicoletti, Sam Orr, Roger T. Peterson, Richard Porter, Steve Potts, Noble Proctor, Chandler Robbins, Will Russell, Fred Sibley, Ted Swem, Fred Tilly, and Hal Wierenga, on whose collective knowledge we have drawn from time to time and in most cases time and time again. We owe a special debt of gratitude to Fred Hamer, who was instrumental in the early development of this book, and to Floyd Wolfarth and Alfred Nicholson, who taught us the magic of hawk-watching and hawk identification.

We also thank Alan Brady, Harry Darrow, Frank Schleicher, and Jimmy Watson, whose photos were included to illustrate key field marks; Gladys Schumacher Donohue, Mary Jane Evans, Steve Hoffman, and Gerry Smith for information about the timetables and distribution of migrating raptors; and Jim Ruos of the Office of Migratory Bird Management, who is very likely the single individual most responsible for the wealth of hawk-migration data available today.

We are grateful to the officers (past and present), the editors, and the members of the Hawk Migration Association of North America for laying the foundation for a book of this nature.

The contributions of Linda Dunne, Pat Sutton, and Joan Walsh to this effort, measured in terms of suggestion (patience), clerical assistance (patience), and perhaps most of all PATIENCE were immeasurable, certainly beyond repayment by any expression of gratitude and beyond any hope of redress.

If singling out one person for a special word of thanks does nothing to detract from the contributions made by others, then we especially thank Linda Mills, whose organizational and editorial skills figured in every aspect of this book.

Introduction

You may never have encountered a field guide to bird identification like this one. Until recently, there was little need for a book of this nature, and the information for it simply did not exist. The standard field guides once defined the frontier of our identification skills and were sufficient. Now the frontier has changed — exceeded the capacities of those guides. The skills and techniques that make it possible to identify hawks in flight are part of a new age of field identification — second-generation birding — and they require a different mode of presentation.

This book has no arrows to highlight distinguishing characteristics. The terse blocks of text characteristic of earlier field guides that described key field marks are here relegated to captions.

This guide is not even designed to be carried into the field (although it may be and should prove useful there). It is meant to be read beforehand. Its development was guided by a single, overriding consideration — the need to communicate subtle identification skills in a way that would be easily understood and remembered. What you will carry into the field with you will be not this book but the information and skills that you will glean from it.

Twenty-three species of raptors are treated, although 38 are found within the geographic limits of the United States and Canada. These 23 species were selected because they constitute the medium- and long-distance raptor migrants (that is, the species most likely to be seen over most of North America). One other species, the Black-shouldered Kite, has been included because of its propensity to wander far outside its normal range in Texas and California.

Eurasian species, such as Steller's Sea Eagle (*Haliaeetus pelagicus*) and the Eurasian Kestrel (*Falco tinnunculus*), which are occasionally recorded on the Aleutian chain off Alaska, or resident species with extremely limited ranges and less propensity for mobility, such as the Hook-billed Kite (*Chondrohierax uncinatus*), have not been included in this book. By eliminating variables we have greatly simplified raptor identification. If you are in areas where these species might occur, then you will need to adjust your expectations accordingly. But there is no need for you to eliminate the Hook-billed Kite from consideration each time you study what may be an immature Red-shouldered Hawk from your favorite New England hawk watch. Geography has already done this work for you.

The various species of raptors have been grouped in this book with an eye toward shared traits and similarity in behavior or appearance. A taxonomist would cringe at the thought of lumping eagles and vultures in one chapter, but a hawk watcher will understand the rationale. At a distance, eagles and vultures look deceptively alike.

Each of the seven identification chapters begins with a basic description of the birds and their traits — those that unite them and those that set them apart from other raptors. Migration is discussed because most raptor observation occurs (and most identification problems arise) during migration.

The section dealing with identification is divided into three parts:

1. A portrayal of each species, its range, and behavior, with perhaps an anecdotal account to illustrate a key characteristic. We include this last because we feel that identification is easier when you understand the nature of the beast somewhat.
2. A detailed description of the identifying field marks (shape, size, plumage, and manner of flight).
3. A section on telling them apart compares and contrasts species of similar appearance.

Each species is illustrated with pen-and-ink drawings that depict age differences and sex differences where they occur. The birds are shown as they would appear to an observer standing below and out of the flight path of the bird — as most hawks are observed. Most guides offer only ventral profiles (views that would be seen only if the birds were directly overhead).

We have intentionally used black-and-white drawings rather than color plates. Raptors are usually identified at distances or altitudes, or under light conditions, that make color difficult or impossible to note. For this reason (and because raptors, on the whole, are variations on the basic theme of black, gray, white, and brown), color rarely figures in identification. Black-and-white illustrations serve well because they closely approximate what an observer will actually see in the field (and field identification is, after all, the subject of this book).

The captions accompanying the illustrations are terse, explicit, and to the point. They were written to facilitate quick referral or to reinforce key distinguishing field marks.

Black-and-white photos were likewise selected because they too best illustrate key points and present images that will be seen from the hawk-watching arena. Portrait shots of perched (or even flying) raptors are beautiful but often bear little resemblance to a bird of the same species flying a quarter of a mile away.

Knowing what you are looking for and when to look for it will greatly help you find whatever you seek. An understanding of hawk migration is invaluable for raptor identification because migration directly relates to the probability of occurrence (knowledge of which is a key tool in the hawk watcher's identification kit). An observer need not consider 38 species (or even 23) whenever a distant bird of prey is being identified. By knowing what species are most likely to be seen at a particular time and place, it is usually possible to reduce the task of identification to a simple choice between this species and that one.

Though hawks migrate over a broad front, certain geographic (and weather) factors (for example, mountain ridges and water barriers) serve to channel and concentrate the flow of birds. People at a number of the key concentration points now operate hawk counts and provide hawk-migration data.

Finally, the text and style of the book probably deserve some comment. This book, unlike many standard field guides, was meant to be read. It was written to be entertaining as well as instructional. A great deal of thought went into selecting words that would fix subjective images in a reader's mind. Humor, and at times an irreverent style, are integral to the text because they convey facts and information in a lively way. We hope you enjoy reading the book.

The identification of birds of prey in flight is a test of skills. Ability increases with knowledge and experience. We are pleased to share our knowledge, and we encourage you to gain in experience — but we do not *challenge* you to do so. The identification of hawks in flight will inevitably challenge you by its very nature. None of us will ever fully conquer that challenge, because another raptor will always be coming along that is just a little bit farther away or a little higher — just slightly out of reach.

Although continental in scope, this guide harbors an unmistakable eastern bias. Given the background of the authors and the long hawk-watching tradition in the East, this was unavoidable. The new and growing popularity of hawk watching in the West is expanding the reach of raptor identification skills. Future editions of this book will be richer for it.

With this in mind, we invite any and all suggestions, information, and criticism that will enhance the value of this book to hawk watchers. Everyone learns, everyone gains, and that is precisely as it should be.

Pete Dunne, David Sibley, and Clay Sutton

The Flight Identification of Raptors

From the Shotgun to the Sublime

There is nothing magical about identifying distant, soaring birds of prey, although more than one casual passerby, observing a throng of hawk watchers in action, has suspected the whole business of having origins in the occult. The skills needed to put a name to a bird that might be little more than a speck on the horizon are firmly rooted in the identification system of the Peterson Field Guides. Raptor identification is the Peterson System refined to accommodate particular needs and constraints, and it has been more than 50 years in the making.

The identification of raptors in flight can be called a discipline. It focuses upon a number of hints and clues all at once, some blatant and obvious, many subjective and transitory. A practiced observer can now identify birds at distances that would once have been considered impossible — not the first time that such an advance has been made.

At one time an ornithologist who wanted to identify a bird would sight along the barrel of a Winchester, pull the trigger, and collect the trophy for study. Birds were then, as they are today, generally skittish and uncooperative creatures, suspicious of ornithologists and their motives, and not inclined to tolerate close or prolonged scrutiny. Shooting the bird overcame the obstacles.

With the bird in hand, the ornithologist could examine it thoroughly and identify it at leisure. Identifications were made on the basis of the color of the gape, the width of the bands on the tail, and the length of the tarsus. This was a *very* workable system, but it had its drawbacks. Most obviously, it was rough on the bird. If the particular problem was identification or the documentation of occurrence, then the shotgun-school approach worked fine, but for the behaviorist it had serious limitations, as it offered insight into the bird's death rather than its life.

Then, too, the shotgun approach was not well suited to urban or suburban environs, and it effectively limited "study" to about 40 yards — the effective range of light shot. Finally, after a good morning in the field, the birdwatcher needed to cart home a lot of dead birds — a morbid task rather than a spiritually uplifting one.

In 1934, a 25-year-old artist and bird enthusiast published a revolutionary book. His name was Roger Peterson, and his *Field Guide to the Birds* was a leap of genius. Its color plates highlighted visible marks that distinguished one species from another in the field. Birds were presented in side profile, as they would appear to someone studying them at a distance through binoculars. Small arrows drew attention to the "trademarks of nature" — the particular traits that differentiated this species from that one — to markings such as wing bars, breast streaks, tail spots, eyelines, eyerings, and so forth.

It was an eminently workable system with much to commend it, but like the shotgun school, it had drawbacks. For one thing, live birds had considerable freedom of movement. Identification often had to be quick, a rapid judgment made under often unfavorable conditions. Sometimes key field marks could not be seen or would be missed because the observer was unfamiliar with the species. The element of certainty diminished. If the observer had second thoughts, there was no way to go to the specimen drawer and recheck — the bird was gone. Another, subtler problem was that the system tended to lock practitioners into a rigid mindset. To this day, some people are skeptical about identifications made when birds are not stationary or do not present a classic side profile. Finally, and perhaps most troublesome, there was the simple fact that the field marks needed to clinch identifications could often be seen only at very close range — sometimes, given the conditions, at closer than shooting range.

When the first hawk-watching pioneers clambered onto the ridge tops and ventured to the tips of peninsulas, they carried with them Roger Peterson's system of identification. Its limitations in the hawk-watching arena immediately became apparent.

On September 17, 1935, Maurice Broun, Hawk Mountain's first curator, recorded 978 Red-shouldered Hawks and 2,175 Broad-winged Hawks from the North Lookout at Hawk Mountain, Pennsylvania. As Maurice noted in his private journal: "I was at my wit's end, differentiating Broad-wingeds from Red-shouldereds."

The problem was a good deal less troublesome than Maurice made it out to be. The birds were *all* Broad-winged Hawks, as everybody knows now (and after a great deal of frustration, Maurice Broun knew it, too). The field mark that had been used to distinguish the two similar-appearing species was the width of the bands on the tail. Maurice had been obliged to make his identifications at distances *too great to let him see the bands on the tail.*

Hawk watching stretched the Peterson System to the limits, and the system fell short. It just didn't work at the distances and angles from which people had to identify fast-moving, migrating birds of prey.

The *new* system of hawk identification developed not overnight but gradually, requiring many seasons and involving a number of keen, attentive minds. Over time, the field marks that did not work were weeded out, and those tailored to the identification of birds of prey in flight were discovered. It was found, for example, that Cooper's Hawks seemed to have large heads and that the head of the otherwise similar Sharp-shinned Hawk appeared small. Red-shouldered Hawks tended to flap more than Red-tailed Hawks, and they frequently flew on the off-wind side of the ridge — the side away from the updraft.

A subtle change in thinking occurred but was at first largely overlooked. A bird was identified as a particular species no longer because it *had* or *showed* this or that particular field mark but because it *seemed* to have this feature or *tended* to exhibit this particular behavior when another species *tended not to do so.* Identifications became more subtle, focused on subjective or transitory clues, and an element of uncertainty became acceptable.

Just because a distinguishing characteristic, a field mark, was not infallible didn't mean that it wasn't a valuable aid to identification. It *was* valuable! It just wasn't definitive; it wasn't a trademark, and it wouldn't stand by itself. The presence of just one or two characteristics did not lead to a concrete identification, and as certainty decreased in relation to distances, the number of field marks needed for a measure of certainty increased. Flight identification of raptors therefore became a science. Today it integrates a number of hints and clues: the rhythm and cadence of a bird's flight; its overall color, shape, and size; plumage characteristics; and behavior under given conditions. All form a composite picture of a bird that may be flying at the limit of conjecture.

Adepts at the Peterson System will find themselves on relatively familiar footing as they edge out onto the hawk watcher's plateau. Many of the field marks used by hawk watchers naturally extend Peterson's leap — the stylized depiction of birds as they appear at a distance. An increase in distance doesn't mean that we must discard the system, but the field marks must reflect what the observer will see (for example, the mark to note is not the wing bar but the shape of the whole wing).

Certain aspects of raptor identification *will* take time to get used to. One example is the reduced emphasis on plumage. For a number of species, particularly buteos, plumage plays a key role in identification (as well as in determining the age, sex, or subspecies of birds). But for the identification of most raptors, plumage characteristics are not as valuable as field marks relating to size, shape, and manner of flight. Color, a key element in the identification of warblers, for example, has only minor significance where raptors are concerned. Hawks are usually flying at distances or under light conditions that make it impossible to discern colors or anything but bold plumage patterns. The drawings in this guide are in black and white because that is how hawks appear in the field: that is how you will see them.

Possibly we should retract, or at least qualify, our initial assertion, that there is nothing magical about hawk identification. If magic is defined as the art of illusion, after all, then the magic inherent in the wind, in the angle of the sun, and in the contours of the earth below can change the shape of birds, so that they look quite different from the way they appear in the hand — so that they even look at times like entirely different species.

A Red-tailed Hawk turning lazy circles in a rising thermal is the very picture of a buteo, wings fully extended, tail fanned. But when the same bird glides to the next thermal, it draws in its wings, closes its tail, and suddenly becomes disconcertingly falconlike. Then, again, riding the updraft off a ridge in a 50-knot wind, with its wings folded flat against its body, a Red-tailed takes on the characteristics of a flying cinderblock. It takes a lot of magic to work such transformations.

The element of distance alone is enough to transform one bird into another. The bird in the bush looks vastly different from the bird in the hand. Individual feathers merge into breast streaks and wing bars. Colors fade but patterns sharpen. When the bird leaves the bush and enters the ozone, even individual features — head, tail, and wings — blur and blend into a composite image and a general shape.

Wing shape to a large extent accounts for the large-headed appearance of Cooper's Hawk and the small-headed look of a Sharp-shinned. The Cooper's Hawk has a wing with a straight leading edge, and the head projects well beyond it. The wing of the Sharp-shinned Hawk juts forward at the wrist, masking the actual extension of the head and making it appear smaller than it actually is.

The wings of a Peregrine Falcon are undeniably long, stiletto thin, and beautifully fluted. But in a full soar, a Peregrine fans its tail so that the outer tail features nearly touch the trailing edge of the wing. The astounding breadth of the tail effectively masks the length of the wing. In general impression and shape, a distinct soaring Peregrine is almost identical to a Broad-winged Hawk — a buteo and a most unlikely candidate for confusion. Raptor identification is concerned not with the actual dimensions or proportions of a bird but with how birds *appear* in flight at a distance. Often, the two aspects are different.

Some people, of course, will still vigorously argue that Cooper's Hawks and Sharp-shinned Hawks don't have proportionately different-sized heads or that tail shape is variable in accipiters and is therefore not a field mark. There is certainly a strong temptation to stay with a safe and familiar method of field identification; people who do will never misidentify a Cooper's Hawk. But by the same token they will never be able to identify one unless they can place it under calipers — a difficult feat in the field.

The flight identification of raptors is a refined blend of identification skills and conjecture, a holistic method. But like its predecessors, this system has its drawbacks. Certainty suffers once again. There is no such thing as 100 percent positive infield identification; an error factor is inherent in every case. Holistic identification is properly a discipline of mind. Its disadvantages are the price we pay for doing what would have seemed impossible just 50 years ago — to identify barely discernible birds and to be right. As in Kierkegaard's leap of faith, we give up something (in this case absolute certainty) in order to gain much more (identifications at near-impossible distances). Such is the nature of the hawk-watching arena, and that is the scope of this book.

Buteos

The Wind Masters

Buteos are a diverse group of medium-to-large hawks that excel in the art of soaring. These are the keen-eyed wind masters, able to tease lift from temperature-troubled air and to soar for long periods on set wings. They are clipper ships of the skies. Unlike accipiters and falcons, which are united by common habitats and hunting methods, buteos exhibit great diversity among species — and even within species.

Rough-legged Hawks and Gyrfalcons will alternate nest ledges in the Brooks Range of Alaska, and Red-shouldered Hawks will share a wooded hillside with a Goshawk in New England. A Swainson's Hawk will course the same willow flats as a Harrier in Wyoming.

Given this diversity of habitats, it should come as no surprise that buteos, as a clan, are versatile hunters and take a variety of prey. Rough-leggeds, Red-taileds, and Ferruginous Hawks can hover-hunt like a Kestrel in search of small rodents. Broad-wingeds will take dragonflies on the wing in the same way that a Mississippi Kite does, and Red-shouldereds can hunt from a perch in the manner of a Goshawk. If there is a niche to be filled by a predator wearing feathers, chances are that a buteo is firmly ensconced in it.

Twelve species of buteos breed in North America north of the

Rio Grande. Many are nonmigratory and are restricted to border regions of the Southwest. Only six species can be called moderate or long-distance migrants and fall within the scope of this book. Subspecies of the Red-tailed Hawk have been included. The Harlan's Hawk, *B. jamaicensis harlani*, the American Ornithologists Union notwithstanding, is very much a long-distance migrant, occupies geographically distinct areas, and differs from a Red-tailed Hawk in plumage and in behavior.

Migration

When most raptor enthusiasts speak of hawk migration, their thoughts turn automatically to buteos — not surprisingly. Geographically speaking, it is the migration that most hawk watchers across the country are in touch with. The spring and fall buteos sweep the continent (in contrast to falcons and accipiters, which hug the coasts). But proximity alone cannot account for the staunch advocacy of "buteo-firsters." If you poll a fair sampling of hawk watchers, a pattern will emerge, a single story with variations relating to an individual, a time, a place, and an event that shifted the focus of a life.

Few people could fail to be impressed by the sight of thousands of Swainson's Hawks rising from the Texas plains in spring or by a dark tornado of swirling, Broad-winged Hawks crossing the Connecticut Valley. Some buteo purists actually take a holiday for most of October after the end of Broad-winged season to wait for the accipiters and falcons to pass before returning to their favorite hawk-watch site. These people count the days, study the weather maps, and wait for the first good cold front in November and the specter of Red-taileds moving beak to tail down the wind-gutted ridge top.

Buteos migrate in a broad, sweeping wave across the continent unless some outside force interferes. Such forces are called "leading lines." A leading line might take the form of large bodies of water, a barrier to migration such as the Great Lakes. When birds heading north or south encounter the shore, they must detour left or right. Concentrations of birds that would otherwise move over a broad front follow the contours of the shoreline (some-times right at the water's edge, sometimes several miles inland, depending on the strength and direction of the wind) and pass over such well-known hawk-watch sites as Whitefish Point, Mich-igan, and Derby Hill, New York, in spring and over Hawk Cliffs, Ontario, and Hawk Ridge (Duluth), Minnesota, in the fall.

An approaching cold front represents another leading line. Hawks moving north in the spring often meet the edge of a front approaching from the northwest. The poor weather and turbu-lence associated with the front act like a barrier. Birds change their course to fly along the edge of the front and congregate along its length, forming a ribbon that advances just ahead of a sweeping weather system.

Mountain ridges also concentrate migrating raptors (particu-larly buteos), but the mechanism is different: ridges attract birds not by blocking their paths but by offering mile upon easy mile of energy-conserving updrafts, a cushion of air that makes a path-way in the sky. Late in the day, migrating raptors will find ther-mals (rising bubbles of warm air generated by uneven heating of the earth's surface) still forming along the southern or western slope of a ridge (where rocks have trapped the day's last sunlight and radiate it back to the heavens long after thermal production has ceased in the valleys). A migration-minded bird simply catches a thermal, rides it upward, sets its wings, and glides, cov-ering ground while expending a minimum of energy.

Thermals are used extensively by all migrating raptors for lift. They are widespread (that is, they are not limited to ridges) and in fact form anywhere that the earth heats at a different rate. A black asphalt parking lot, for example, heats more rapidly than the surrounding lawn. When the air lying over the surface of the lot becomes warmer than the surrounding air by as little as one or two degrees, it rises and forms a thermal. On days when ther-mals are strong and widespread, hawks prefer them to an updraft off a ridge as a way of gaining lift. Ridge updrafts are used prin-cipally on days of heavy cloud cover (days when thermal produc-tion is restricted) and on days when strong winds strike a ridge at an angle and create a good updraft. Coincidentally, strong winds also disrupt thermal production by causing air to mix too rapidly.

If a ridge is not headed in the direction in which a migrating buteo wants to travel, is not continuous, or has contours with difficult oxbows — or if the landscape is dotted with isolated hills or rock formations not linked by a geological ribbon — raptors may still be drawn to the handy updrafts that these formations create and may use the updrafts as if they were thermals. The birds will circle over the updraft, ride it aloft, and then head off at a glide angle calculated to take them to a distant thermal or, very often, to another opportune updraft farther along the route.

Buteo migration is protracted and may fairly be said to be occurring over some part of North America during every month of the year.

The vanguard of the fall migration of Broad-wingeds filters through New England during mid to late August; the peak flights occur near September 10 on the north shore of Lake Ontario and near September 15 in Massachusetts. September 17 is the magic date at Hawk Mountain, Pennsylvania. Little is heard about the tide of birds until they reach Texas and cross the Rio Grande about two weeks later.

By the third week in October, the buteos are advancing on Hawk Ridge (Duluth). By midmonth, Hawk Mountain is under the spell of the Red-shouldered Hawk push, to be followed by the big Red-tailed Hawk migration, which comes before or after November 1, whenever the period's major cold front hits. Just as warm fronts stimulate movement in the spring, cold fronts produce large movements in the fall.

Immature birds precede adults in the fall; adults return earlier in the spring. During fall migration the first day after the passage of a cold front is best for viewing large numbers of birds on the eastern ridges, though at coastal or peninsula hawk-watch sites, often the second (or, if you are fortunate, the third) day of offshore winds gives the best results as more and more birds gather along the coastline.

The fall buteo flights continue in pulses, triggered by each successive cold front, growing progressively smaller and smaller un-

til, by late December and early January, a massive cold front, with
a heavy snowfall farther north, is needed to produce even a scat-
tering of late-moving adult birds — small reward for a day's cold
vigil.

In mid-February, at the first sign of thaw, Rough-legged
Hawks begin moving north past south shore Great Lakes sites,
along with rebounding Red-tailed Hawks, whose migration
peaks with a rush during the first part of March. Red-shouldereds
follow, peaking by early April, just before the first Broad-wingeds
reach New England.

The Broad-winged (and Swainson's) hawks surge across the
Rio Grande at the end of March. Their cresting wave reaches New
England by April 17 and consists of adults. Subadults follow more
leisurely, peaking in late May. Stragglers, bizarre-looking birds
with plumages ravaged by travel and molt, continue to wander
north as late as the first week in July. They are still moving north
as the first birds of autumn are heading south.

Identification

Buteo identification, like the identification of all birds in flight,
relies on the integration of a number of hints and clues before a
judgment is made, but it tends to be more traditional in scope.
Birders who have grown familiar with the system of "immutable
field marks" will find themselves on familiar ground here. Accordingly, buteo identification offers an easy point of departure for a
walk down unfamiliar paths.

Unlike accipiter identification, which depends on relative shape
and proportions, and falcon identification, which emphasizes
shape and flight characteristics, buteo identification draws heavily
upon plumage, for several reasons.

First, buteos are large birds of open areas. The observer viewing
them has ample time to note and absorb even small details of
plumage.

Second, buteos soar a great deal without flapping as often as
falcons or accipiters, and one distant, soaring bird looks pretty
much like another. Certain species do tend to hold their wings in
a particular way (and this feature is a useful aid to identification),

but wing position is highly variable and changes in response to wind and weather and in response to the task at hand. For example, Red-tailed Hawks usually fly with a moderate dihedral. But some individuals show a very pronounced uplifting of the wings. In high winds the same hawk may hold its wings perfectly flat or, if it is using a very light updraft off a ridge, it may actually droop its wings slightly in the manner of a Red-shouldered Hawk.

Third and most important, however, the marks of plumage are reliable and are bold enough in most cases to be seen at great distances. Dark-phase birds, of course, present their own special set of problems. But if the flight identification of raptors is a subjective science, it is also an opportunistic one: if plumage offers a quick and easy route to correct identifications, why take a hard one?

The Generic Buteo

The typical buteo is a medium-to-large raptor with a heavy body and broadly proportioned wings and short tail. The wing tips are generally blunt but sometimes appear tapered. The back is dark, often mottled. Underparts are usually light, with varying amounts of dark streaking, barring, and patches on the underwings and body. (Note: a bird will occasionally be extensively and uniformly dark on the body, the underwing linings, the entire underwing, or the entire underparts.)

Buteos soar frequently and use thermals extensively for lift. They are quick to exploit the updraft off a ridge, particularly on cloudy days when thermals are few. Wing beats are slow, heavy, and methodical and often occur in a series of three to five, followed by a glide.

Red-tailed Hawk

The Red-tailed Hawk is a large, stocky hawk of woodlots, fields, alpine meadows, prairies, and roadsides all across the country — the classic buteo. In terms of weight, it is the largest eastern buteo. Only the western Ferruginous Hawk is heavier. Only it and the Rough-legged Hawk exceed the Red-tailed in measurements.

Red-taileds are the epitome of a buteo, a study in functional diversity. Their hunting habits and habitat preferences are so varied that to single out just one characteristic is to do them an injustice.

Red-taileds can hover-hunt like Kestrels, steadfastly hang motionless in the wind, stoop with single-mindedness, and perch-hunt with consummate finesse. This versatility makes the Red-tailed Hawk as much at home hunting *Microtus* (voles) in South Amboy, New Jersey, as it is hunting pheasant in South Dakota. And although small rodents are the mainstay of the bird's diet throughout most of its range, the Red-tailed Hawk, like many predators, is highly opportunistic. Anything readily available and catchable is an odds-on favorite to become prey. Any furred, feathered, or scaled creature that is smaller than a groundhog and turns its back on a meal-minded Red-tailed Hawk might safely be said to be courting a shortcut toward the cosmic.

The Red-tailed Hawk has demonstrated an amazing ability to acclimate itself to the world of man's making. The agricultural practices of the Northeast, which cleared bottomland and left hilltops forested, provided ideal habitat. The woodlots harbored the bird's stick nest, and the fields provided a surfeit of prey.

The Eisenhower administration's lasting gift to mobile America, the interstate highway system, further benefited Red-taileds by creating mile upon straight-cut mile of ideal hunting and wintering habitat from the originally unusable forest. The wood's edge provides hunting perches; the grassy roadsides and wide center divisions are ideal habitat for small rodents.

As propitious for Red-taileds as the leveling of trees in the East was the planting of them (or their creosote-soaked remains) in the West. First the telegraph, then the telephone created miles of well-spaced hunting perches.

One subspecies of Red-tailed Hawk or another ranges from central Alaska to Hudson Bay, across most of eastern Canada, and south through Mexico. In winter, the bird retreats to territories south of Canada and the northern plains states.

A   B   C

Buteos: soaring immatures of all species, backlit. Compare size, patterns of wing translucence, wing shape. Adults of all species have significantly shorter tails than immatures, with shorter, broader wings.

(A) Red-tailed Hawk: well-rounded wings pushed forward at wrist, bulging outer secondaries, dark patagial mark and belly band, light chest, and pale inner primaries.

(B) Swainson's Hawk: long, evenly curved wings with pointed tips; only four emarginated primaries; all flight feathers dark.

(C) Ferruginous Hawk: long, straight-edged, and rather pointed wings; extremely pale; all flight feathers translucent; body strikingly white.

(D) Rough-legged Hawk: long, straight-edged, broad-tipped wings; black belly and wrist patches; otherwise rather pale, translucent primaries.

(E) Red-shouldered Hawk: short wings pushed well forward, with square-cut tips; long tail; translucent slash across wing tip; evenly streaked body.

(F) Broad-winged Hawk: small, with short, pointed wings; only four emarginated primaries; short tail; translucent inner primaries; streaking concentrated on breast.

IDENTIFICATION. Study this bird closely: a working familiarity with the Red-tailed provides a reference point for the measurement and comparison of all other buteos. This sturdy raptor shows a wide range in size. The largest Red-taileds can seem almost as large as an eagle and weigh twice as much as smaller birds. Individuals differ in proportions as well. There are long-tailed and long-winged birds (usually immatures) and stocky, short-tailed ones (adults).

Except for their tails, adults and immatures are very similar in plumage: brown to gray-brown above and light below, with varying amounts of speckling and streaking. The underparts appear dirty on immatures; adults often show a rosy blush across the chest.

A

B

Dark-phase buteo adults gliding. Dark extremes — blackish body, head, and underwing coverts — are illustrated, but all species are variable and can be rufous or mottled. Immatures can also be dark and provide more variation. Flight feathers always appear in light phase, upper side similar to light phase. Minor variations in plumage may be difficult to see, and identification must often be based on size and shape and range.

(A) Red-tailed Hawk: primaries and secondaries are pale gray with faint barring; tail red (adult) or brown with fine bars (immature). See also Harlan's Hawk.

(B) Ferruginous Hawk: primaries and secondaries unbarred white, with tiny black tips on primaries (gray on immature); tail (mixed white, gray, and reddish) may show faint bars; undertail coverts pale rufous; white comma inside black one.

(C) Rough-legged Hawk: primaries and secondaries silvery with faint barring; extensive black tips on all; tail barred (adult) or pale gray (immature).

(D) Swainson's Hawk: dark flight feathers with pale spot at base of primaries; pale undertail coverts.

(E) Broad-winged Hawk: all primaries and secondaries dark-tipped; tail broadly banded black and white (adult) or brown with several fine bars (immature).

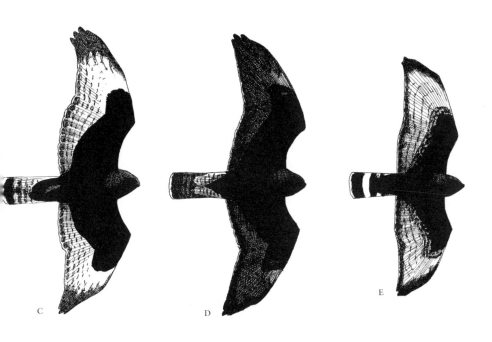

C

D

E

Only adult birds have a red tail (it is assumed gradually during the bird's second year). Even dark-phase birds and the very pale Krider's form (both rare in the East) show a reddish tail. Only the Alaskan Harlan's form lacks the color entirely; its tail is gray or white. (See **Subspecies** below.) Immature birds have finely barred brown tails that show white at the base.

The length of the tail is variable. Adults have very short tails, and the tails of immatures may appear as long as that of any Red-shouldered Hawk. The bright red tail of an adult is virtually diagnostic in the East, permits confusion only with the Ferruginous Hawk in the West, and is visible at a tremendous distance. *Caution: when backlit by the sun, the tails of Ospreys and immature Red-shouldered Hawks take on a reddish cast.* A male Kestrel also has a red tail, but a Kestrel and a Red-tailed Hawk are unlikely to be confused.

The long, broad, and round-tipped wings appear bulging and muscular, like the overdeveloped arms of a weight lifter. The limbs of other buteos appear straighter and smoother. In a full soar, the hand is often angled forward, as if the wing had been broken and had healed improperly.

Red-taileds are very white below. Most eastern birds have distinct belly bands, perhaps the bird's best field mark. Sometimes the band is faint (consisting of neat, fine streaking); sometimes it resembles the stroke of a black paintbrush drawn across clean white canvas. It is usually found across the middle (belly) of the underparts, although it sometimes rides higher (on the chest) or farther back (near the legs). Wherever minor variation places it, the belly band is a good field mark and visible at great distances. Even veteran hawk watchers look for it to clinch a distant identification.

Adult (*left*) and immature Red-tailed Hawk (*right*). Adult has shorter, broader wings; shorter tail; slightly blacker markings; missing or uneven flight feathers; darker (opaque) flight feathers.

Adult Red-tailed (*left*) with adult Red-shouldered (*right*).

A

B

Red-tailed Hawk, underside.

(A) Immature

(B) Adult

Large and broadly proportioned; shape variable, but generally wings are rounded and show bulging outer secondaries. Body broad and heavy. Note dark patagium, dark comma, and light area in between that shows as white headlights on approaching bird. Heavily streaked belly band, white chest. Typical individuals of Eastern race (*B. J. borealis*) are shown; variations within this subspecies include birds with heavy black belly band and heavily spotted underwing coverts as well as some with very few dark markings on body, as on Krider's (see p. 21).

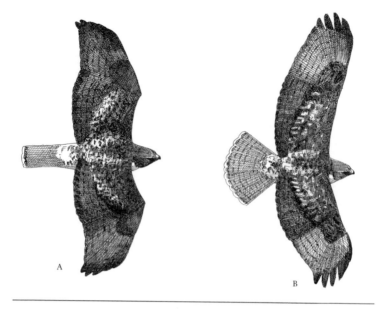

Red-tailed Hawk, upperside.
  (A) Adult
  (B) Immature
Mottled dark brown, with five distinct patches of white speckling on greater
coverts, scapulars, and uppertail coverts. Adult shows reddish tail with black
subterminal band; immature has brown tail with many fine bars. Note pale
inner primaries on immature; lack of pigment here produces patch that looks
translucent when seen from below. This patch is less prominent on adults,
which are generally darker above.

The band's absence does nothing but accentuate another excellent field mark, the white chest. In the East, immature Red-shouldered Hawks, Broad-winged Hawks (and Swainson's Hawks),
and adult Rough-legged Hawks will have streaking on the chest
(or at least down the sides of the chest). Even an immature light-
phase Rough-legged Hawk has a dirty chest, not a white one. In
the East, a distant buteo with a clean, white chest is almost certainly a Red-tailed Hawk; in the West, it might be a Ferruginous
Hawk.

The underwings of a Red-tailed Hawk are usually more
splotched or patterned than those of other buteos. Two distinc-

Phases of Red-tailed Hawk. There is extensive variation. The five views shown here suggest the range, but virtually any combination of characters is possible.

(A) Adult *B. J. krideri*: extremely pale; body and underwing mostly unstreaked; head pale; tail mostly white with pinkish wash and dark band near tip; conspicuous translucent patches on inner primaries.

(B) Immature *B. j. borealis*: the typical Eastern Red-tailed; white breast; distinct belly band and patagial mark.

(C) Adult *B. j. calurus*: the typical Western Red-tailed, usually more heavily marked than *borealis,* with dark throat; rusty streaking on breast and underwing coverts; several dark bands near tail tip.

(D) Adult *B. j. calurus,* rufous phase: as shown in view (C), but all light areas replaced by rufous and all markings still apparent.

(E) Adult *B. j. calurus,* black phase: body and underwing entirely blackish, no markings apparent. All flight feathers remain as in light phase.

A   B   C

D   E

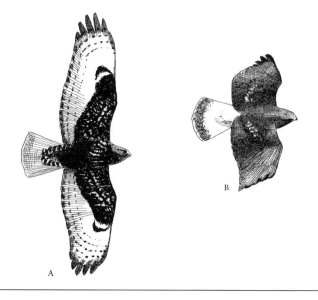

A

B

Harlan's Hawk (*B. j. harlani*). Average bird is smaller, slimmer than other Red-taileds, with longer tail and primaries, straighter-edged wings. Body and underwing coverts always dark with white spotting (A), contrasting with silvery flight feathers. Upperside (B) dark with a few white spots on coverts. Rump white and tail white, with dusky mottling near tip. The light extreme is illustrated. Other birds have tail entirely mottled. Immatures probably not distinguishable from other dark Red-taileds but always dark with white spotting and checkering on body and underwing coverts; tail banded as on other Red-taileds.

tive marks are useful at close range: the bold "commas" located at the wrist (carpal area) of the wing and the bold dark line running along the leading edge of the arm (patagium). The commas are very faint on the Red-shouldered Hawk and the Broad-winged Hawk and are replaced by large black patches on light-phase Rough-leggeds. Only the western Swainson's and Ferruginous hawks share this mark with the Red-tailed. The dark patagium is unique to Red-taileds. The Ferruginous Hawk may show a faint shading on the patagium but never a distinct black line.

    Seen head-on, the area between the comma and the patagial line appears as a white patch on the leading edge of the wing.

When a flying bird approaches, these areas on its wings resemble a set of landing lights on an aircraft.

Dark-phase birds are common in western states and rare in the East. Dark-phase birds are usually reddish brown (not black) on the body and underwing linings. A belly band, darker than the rest of the underparts, is usually present, and adults still have a red tail.

The Red-tailed Hawk is a master soarer and on days when there is good lift may not flap at all. When soaring, the bird usually carries its wings slightly lifted in a dihedral less pronounced than that of a Golden Eagle, Turkey Vulture, Swainson's Hawk, or Northern Harrier. (Since a Red-tailed is heavier than a Harrier, Swainson's Hawk, or Turkey Vulture, it does not rock in flight.) A Rough-legged Hawk also has a dihedral, but the wing configuration is more hunched at the shoulders and flattened at the hands. In contrast, the dihedral of a Red-tailed Hawk is flat along the shoulders and uplifted along the hands, like that of a Ferruginous Hawk.

In level point-to-point flight, the wing beat of a Red-tailed is slow, heavy, and powerful but fluid and oddly shallow. The beat appears evenly distributed along the length of the wing. In high winds, if the bird is blown off center, it will right itself by flexing a wing; Red-shouldereds and Broad-wingeds will right themselves with a choppy series of wing beats.

Red-taileds flap a good deal less than all hawks but the Ferruginous. When they soar, their bearing is heavier and their turns slower, more methodical.

Red-taileds are capable of hover-hunting in place, but only the Red-tailed and Ferruginous hawks are capable of kiting — holding themselves immobile into the wind on set wings like a kite tugging against a string. Any bird that loses its forward momentum and holds fast over a spot east of Missouri may with virtual certainty be identified as a Red-tailed Hawk.

SUBSPECIES OF RED-TAILED HAWK. In the case of most raptors, identification stops at the species level. In a few cases it is possible to identify birds (particularly adults) at the subspecies level with a fair level of confidence. The Red-tailed Hawk is one example — or seven, if you prefer: *Buteo jamaicensis borealis, B. j. harlani, B. j. calurus, B. j. krideri, B. j. fuertesi, B. j. alascensis,* and *B. j. umbrinus.*

Thus far our discussion has focused largely on the Eastern Red-tailed (*B. j. borealis*), the generic Red-tailed. This section will consider three other forms: the Western Red-tailed (*B. j. calurus*), Krider's Red-tailed (*B. j. krideri*), and Harlan's Hawk (*B. j. harlani*). All three of these subspecies have distinctive peculiarities of plumage. All are bound by their migratory tendencies and propensity to wander outside their normal ranges. Omitted are Fuertes' Red-tailed (*B. j. fuertesi*), of the Southwest; the Alaskan Red-tailed (*B. j. alascensis*); and the Florida Red-tailed (*B. j. umbrinus*) because of their restricted distribution, their sedentary natures, or their fundamental similarity to the generic Red-tailed.

Observers should bear in mind that very many individual Red-taileds (particularly immatures) cannot be relegated to subspecies. Members of each subspecies may interbreed, and intergrades occur with interesting combinations of traits.

HARLAN'S HAWK. Formerly regarded as a separate species (*B. harlani*), the bird was reclassed as a subspecies of the Red-tailed Hawk in 1973 by the American Ornithologists Union, which exercises authority in such matters. Contemporary thought notwithstanding, some students of raptordom are awaiting a retrial. There are, to many minds, several subspecies of Red-tailed Hawk, and Harlan's Hawk is a bird that doesn't quite fit the mold.

Harlan's occupies a select and limited range. It breeds in the coniferous forests and bogs of southern Alaska and British Columbia. Its winter territory was historically the tallgrass prairies of Kansas, Missouri, and Oklahoma (a few birds appearing in portions of Texas and Arkansas and as far west as Arizona). Its migration is extensive.

If Harlan's is a Red-tailed, then it is invariably a dark-phase Red-tailed. The typical adult Harlan's Hawk is brownish black with white speckling or mottling on the dorsal surface, chest, and underwings. The flight feathers of adults are silvery white, un-marked, or perhaps slightly barred. The bird virtually replicates a dark-phase Rough-legged Hawk.

The tails of adults are highly variable but streaked, never barred. Some individuals show a brilliant white tail above, tipped with a diffuse brown-black terminal band that recalls an immature Golden Eagle. Other adults have dark brown tails with white streaks scattered throughout their length that dissolve into a black terminal band. More commonly the tail patterns fall between these extremes and show variations on the theme of dirty white or gray with dark streaks and a dark tip.

Immature Harlan's Hawks are not always separable from other dark Red-taileds. Differences are matters of degree, and hybrids occur. Immature Harlan's may nevertheless be distinguished if the observer is willing to allow a generous margin for error.

The typical immature *harlani* is similar to the adult but has spotting, particularly on the upperwing coverts and upper chest. A light chest and throat are always present, but the degree of spotting elsewhere is variable. Some lightly spotted birds appear very dark at a distance; other heavily spotted birds seem gray. The undertail coverts are distinctly barred, black on white, and appear quite pale on some birds.

The tail of the immature is always finely barred — just like that of a typical immature dark-phase Red-tailed Hawk. Flight feathers, too, are finely barred, so that the underwings appear a tarnished silver and duskier than those of adults.

Adult dark-phase Western Red-taileds are easily distinguished from Harlan's. Rufous-phase *calurus* is, quite simply, a bird of a different color. Black-phase *calurus* lacks the pronounced mottling typical of Harlan's, and the flight feathers have more barring and are darker overall, not silver. The tails of adult Western Red-taileds are red.

Immature Western Red-taileds are typically darker overall than immature Harlan's Hawks, with more barring on the wings and tail and less spotting (or none at all). Plumages, however, overlap in too many respects to differentiate Harlan's reliably from other dark Red-taileds. Other factors play an important role here.

Harlan's Hawks on the average are smaller than a typical Western Red-tailed. The bird is slimmer, more slightly built, and rangier. The body is slender and tubular, the neck longer and snakier. Immature Harlan's appear to have a distinctly longer tail.

When gliding into a wind, or riding ridges, Harlan's looks more distinctly angular than the standard Red-tailed. The flight feathers, frequently drawn back, make the bird's wings look pointy. The angles of the wing are more severe.

Taken together, the long tail, long neck, and thin, angular wings give the bird a distinct resemblance to a Rough-legged Hawk. Harlan's might be said to occupy, in shape and plumage, a middle ground between the clean-limbed Rough-legged Hawk and the stocky Red-tailed.

Harlan's Hawk hovers and kites in the wind exactly like a Red-tailed and shows a preference for ridge hunting — hanging low, scanning the flat landscape, with its head constantly swiveling from side to side (and even turning to look behind the bird), much like that of a Rough-legged Hawk. The call of the bird is slightly higher pitched and more monosyllabic than that of the average Red-tailed.

WESTERN RED-TAILED. The typical western subspecies, the counterpart to *B. j. borealis* in the East, breeds north to Alaska and east to — well, nobody is quite sure. As a migrant and wintering bird, it regularly occurs along the Atlantic seaboard.

There are three basic color phases of *calurus,* which for reference and simplicity, might be labeled light phase, rufous phase, and black phase. Variations are many.

Light-phase *calurus* birds are essentially a darker, more heavily printed version of the generic, or Eastern, Red-tailed. Upperparts often have a warmer, rufous cast; underparts are boldly patterned. Typical Red-tailed field marks are vivid and sharply defined. Rusty streaks commonly occur on the breast and legs. The red tails of adults are finely barred in contrast to those of Eastern Red-taileds.

Red-phase *calurus* individuals are, overall, a rich, warm reddish brown, cinnamon and chocolate. Typical Red-tailed markings are visible. The reader should bear in mind, however, that both

Swainson's Hawks and Ferruginous Hawks also have an erythrismal phase.

On black-phase *calurus* birds the typical Red-tailed markings are invisible. The flight feathers are white with some barring (like those of typical Red-taileds).

In shape, little distinguishes the Western Red-tailed from Eastern birds. Western Red-taileds appear to have wings that taper somewhat more than those of typical Eastern Red-taileds, a trait that other western buteos seem to share.

Western Red-taileds also hold their wings differently. Whereas the wings of Eastern Red-taileds jut upward in a sharply angled V-shaped dihedral, Western birds usually show a U-shaped dihedral.

KRIDER'S RED-TAILED HAWK. The palest of the several Red-tailed subspecies — even paler than the Ferruginous Hawk, a species to which it is superficially more similar — Krider's is a prairie Red-tailed breeding in the southern prairie provinces of Canada. It winters in the southern plains states south through Texas. Vagrants have appeared as far east as Cape May, New Jersey, in the fall. The bird is probably annual in Florida in winter.

In size and shape, Krider's is a typical Red-tailed, but its plumage sets it apart. From below, the bird is *white* except for gray to black wing tips and pale (tan to brown) patagial marks and commas. The head, too, is white. The tail ranges from white to tan.

The dorsal surface of the bird is stunning and distinctive. The upperwing coverts and back are mottled white and tan. The tail ranges from white to rufous wash, with a narrow, dark subterminal band.

Immatures resemble adults but have tails that are tan and finely barred.

On adult or immature birds, large white upperwing patches situated on the flight feathers just short of the slotted wing tips are distinctive and obvious. Apart from its pale tail, Krider's is, pure and simple, a Red-tailed with large white patches on the upperparts — tail and wing tips.

The light-phase Ferruginous Hawk has the same set of distinc-

A

B

Red-shouldered Hawk, underside.
  (A) Immature
  (B) Adult
Medium-sized, rather stocky; wings clean-edged, rounded. In all plumages
the translucent slash just inside the black primary tips is prominent. Bird is
otherwise distinguished from Broad-winged by larger size, broader wing tips;
immature also by uniformly streaked breast, adult also by narrow white bands
on tail, barred primaries and secondaries, rusty barring on wing coverts.

tive field marks, but the wing patches are more restricted. The
white does not extend down the length of the flight feather but
is confined to the feather base. The wing patch on Krider's forms
large rectangular patches which encompass the outer flight feathers. The Ferruginous Hawk also differs from Krider's in size and
particularly in shape.

Red-shouldered Hawk

The Red-shouldered Hawk is a forest buteo — the buteo that
thinks it is an accipiter. It is at home on the wooded hillsides of

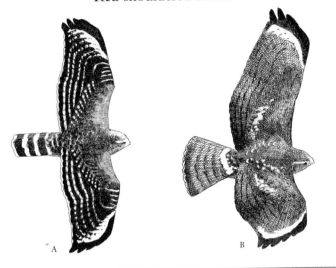

Red-shouldered Hawk, upperside.
  (A) Adult
  (B) Immature
Adult strikingly patterned, with rufous shoulders and black-and-white
barring. White crescent on wing tip produces translucent window below.
Immature brown with some white spotting on coverts, scapulars, and
uppertail coverts; bold tawny crescent across wing tip distinguishes this
species from all others.

New England and in the deep hardwood swamps of the Old
South. Although there is an isolated West Coast population, this
bird is typically more an easterner.

The swamp hawk is an eclectic predator. During warmer
months, it seeks cold-blooded prey ranging from insects to reptiles. During the winter, rodents become the bird's dietary mainstay but are frequently supplemented by small birds. The talons
of the Red-shouldered Hawk are much smaller than those of the
Red-tailed Hawk, and so prey larger than a gray or red squirrel is
the exception rather than the rule.

Red-shouldereds are secretive and do not favor the open areas
frequented by so many buteos. In winter, the Red-shouldered
Hawk may occasionally sit on the sunny edge of fields as a Red-

tailed Hawk does. But like summer birds, winter Red-shouldereds
are most often heard and not seen.

IDENTIFICATION. The Red-shouldered Hawk is a medium-sized
buteo about three-quarters the size of a Red-tailed Hawk in
flight. The body is slighter than that of a Red-tailed and is
slimmer and tube shaped. Overall it appears slimmer, trimmer,
more clean-cut. If the Red-tailed Hawk is just plain folk, the Red-
shouldered Hawk is gentry.

The Red-shouldered Hawk is beautiful. Adult plumage is striking: body and underwings are chestnut, and flight feathers and
tail are boldly striped with black and white. The upperwing coverts (shoulders) are rusty, hence the bird's name. The smaller adult
Broad-winged Hawk is similar but lacks rust-colored shoulders
and has a tail that is broadly banded. At close range, the white
bands on the tail of a Red-shouldered Hawk resemble thin chalk
lines on a blackboard.

Immature birds lack the distinctive plumage of adults. Young
Red-shouldereds are brown above (sparsely mottled with white)
and cream-colored below with streaking, particularly heavy on the
chest.

The wings are long, narrow, and clean-edged and lack the muscular bulges seen on the Red-tailed. The leading edge is straight.
The trailing edge curves gently (usually on adults) or not at all
(usually on immatures). The wing tip is cut straight on an angle.
Seen from below, the wing of a Red-shouldered Hawk suggests

Immature Red-shouldered Hawk in full soar.

a long, rectangular plank. The entire wing juts forward when the bird is in a full soar, as if it were reaching out, arms wide, to embrace something.

The tail on immatures is long for a buteo but still broad. Adults have rather short tails, but because Red-shouldereds have narrow, planklike wings, even high-soaring adult birds may appear long-tailed (although the impression disappears at close range). The tail is blunt, not notched (unless the bird is molting).

The best field identification mark for Red-shouldered Hawks is the crescent-shaped "stained-glass window" that contours the tip of each wing. The absence of pigmentation near the base of the outer flight feathers allows light to pass through. The "window" is tawny on immatures, white on adults, and visible at great distances from above or below. *Caution: other buteos may show translucent oval or rectangular patches on the wings (usually found on the inner primaries or secondaries). These are not "windows."* Only rarely will a Red-tailed or Broad-winged Hawk display a tawny, crescent-shaped window, and the reason is usually the molt of one or more outer primaries (which generally occurs only in late spring or early summer).

Immature Red-shouldereds are heavily streaked on the chest. Young Red-taileds are streaked across the middle but are clean-chested. Young Broad-wingeds are more heavily streaked down the sides of the face, throat, and sides but also have very clean chests. Red-shouldereds have relatively unmarked underwings. If a comma is present, it will be faint.

The Red-shouldered is animated, high-strung, and considerably more active in flight than a Red-tailed. In point-to-point flight, the wing beat is quicker and lacks the fluid quality of a Red-tailed's. The beat appears stiff as if the bird were batting the air. The flight looks like that of a buteo trying to imitate an accipiter. *Rule of thumb: if you have a bird at a distance that you initially identify as a Goshawk, and if after closer study it turns out to be a buteo, it is a Red-shouldered Hawk.*

Because the Red-shouldered Hawk weighs less than a Red-tailed, it is less able to buck high winds. When it is thrown off balance, it will right itself by beating frantically. A Red-tailed will

Top to bottom: immature Broad-winged, immature Cooper's, adult male Harrier, all soaring.

simply flex a wing or make one or two methodical corrective flaps.

Red-shouldereds typically soar on wings that have a slight downward droop, as if the bird were cupping the air.

Broad-winged Hawk

If a hawk watcher in Massachusetts were asked about the best time to watch hawks, the answer would probably be: "Broad-wingeds peak about the fifteenth of September." If the same person were asked whether hawks eat during migration, the reply would be: "Probably not. There are just too many Broad-wingeds moving together at any time for the birds to find anything to eat."

In many places, hawk watching is the same thing as watching the Broad-winged Hawk. And why not? The annual spring and fall exodus of the Broad-winged must be one of the greatest spectacles in nature. Even veterans who have seen it for many seasons leave the lookout on the big day speechless with awe.

The Broad-winged is a small buteo of deciduous woodlands. It ranges west to the tree-poor prairie states and north to the beginnings of the evergreen forests. The bird is retiring and docile by raptorial standards. It is a perch hunter of the deep woods. Though it will take small mammals and a few birds, cold-blooded animals are its mainstay: insects, frogs, snakes, salamanders, and toads. For this reason Broad-wingeds leave early in the fall and return late in the spring. Unlike the Red-tailed and Red-shouldered hawks, which merely vacate northern portions of their range and withdraw deeper into southern portions, the Broad-winged population (except for stragglers and a wintering Florida population) fully vacates its North American breeding territories and relocates in Central and South America.

In migration, the bird is highly gregarious, and this quality gives it a large following in the hawk-watching community. Broad-wingeds migrate in flocks ranging from several individuals to several thousand birds that travel across the country seeking out thermals, the rising currents of warm air that provide lift. A flock of Broad-wingeds circling within a thermal is called a kettle in the mid-Atlantic states and a boil in New York for the resemblance of the milling airborne birds to water bubbling on the stove. The sight of several thousand milling hawks is undeniably awesome, and it is small wonder that the bird has so many followers.

The reputation of a season's migration is linked with the success of the Broad-winged push. At gatherings, hawk watchers recall time and again the legendary flights of 10,000 birds, but big day counts of from 3,000 to 5,000 are more common in the East. Large counts in south Texas, however, start at 10,000 birds and run as high as an estimated 100,000.

IDENTIFICATION. Broad-winged Hawks are small, chunky, stubby buteos hardly larger than a crow. Adults are easily recognized by the broad black-and-white bands on the tail; adult Red-shouldereds have narrow white bands. Immatures are brown above, creamy below, and heavily streaked on the face, throat, sides, and belly — in other words, they are not unlike several other species of immature raptors.

The wings, in a full soar, are short and broad. They are held at almost a perfect right angle to the body. The lines are clean, without abrupt bumps or bulges. Both the leading and trailing edges taper toward a point, in the fashion of a lancet arch. But when the bird is gliding, in a partial tuck, the wings curve back along

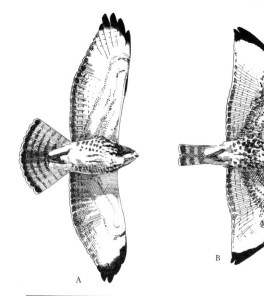
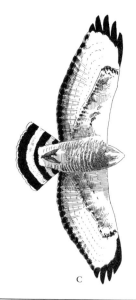

Broad-winged Hawk, underside.
  (A) Typical immature
  (B) Heavily marked immature
  (C) Adult
Small, chunky; wings broad, clean-edged, pointed. Tail broad when fanned in soar but narrow and square-tipped in glide. Immatures differentiated from Red-shouldereds by shape, lack of pale window, and streaking and spotting concentrated on side breast and flanks (so that breast remains relatively clean), sometimes forming belly band as on (B). Underwing unmarked white (A) to heavily spotted (B). Tail bands variable but may be helpful in individuals with conspicuous dark subterminal band as in (A); Red-shouldereds normally have uniform bands. Adults have faint whitish markings and a conspicuous black border on underwing and show one broad white band across tail.

the leading edge and become straight along the trailing edge, like the blade of a paring knife.

During a soar, the tail opens very wide, so that both it and the already stubby wings appear shorter. When the tail is closed, it is very narrow, very long, and very unlike the tail of a buteo. It is usually notched and often flares outward slightly at the tip. When the tail is closed, it suggests that of a Sharp-shinned Hawk.

Broad-winged Hawk, upperside.
  (A) Adult
  (B) Immature
Adult, uniformly brownish with banded tail. Immature very similar to Red-shouldered Hawk but lacks tawny crescent; may show pale inner primaries, light brown tail.

The streaking on the underparts of the body of an immature Broad-winged is normally heavy along the side of the face and down the sides of the throat, spreading out over the belly and often giving the appearance of a belly band. The chest is frequently unmarked or very faintly marked (unlike that of the immature Red-shouldered Hawk).

Seen at close range, the width of the subterminal band on the tail can help distinguish immature Broad-winged Hawks from immature Red-shouldereds. On a Broad-winged Hawk, the dark subterminal band is much darker and wider than the other bands on the tail. On the Red-shouldered Hawk, the band is not noticeably different.

The underwings of both immature and (particularly) adult Broad-wingeds are very clean and white. The whiteness is accentuated by the broad, dark outer border of the wing extending from the tip back along the trailing edge. The impression is that of a white piece of canvas bordered by a black frame.

Broad-wingeds are confirmed users of thermals, and during migration, they travel in large groups. In the East, a large flock of buteos automatically means Broad-winged. In the West, Swainson's Hawks and Mississippi Kites also migrate in large, thermal-exploiting flocks (as do Sandhill Cranes). Though all species of raptors will use thermals to gain altitude in migration, the Broad-winged Hawk seems to depend more on thermals than most. Flights commence in the morning as soon as thermals begin to form and shut down soon after thermal production ceases in late afternoon.

In between thermals, Broad-wingeds will pump and glide, and in a high wind, they will flap to maintain balance. The wing beat is quick, stiff throughout its length, and choppy, not loose or snappy and not heavy or labored.

In a soar, the wings are held horizontally and *flat,* not uplifted or drooped. In a glide between thermals (when wings are pulled in slightly) or when the bird is using an updraft off a ridge, the wings may be angled stiffly downward.

When the bird is seen head-on, as it sometimes is on ridge watches, the bright yellow cere around the base of the bill is often visible at a great distance.

Dark-phase Broad-wingeds are extremely uncommon in the East and perhaps number as few as 1 in 50,000. The frequency of occurrence hardly makes these birds a vexing problem (particularly since dark-phase individuals will be just one in a large flock and very, very obvious).

Swainson's Hawk

The Swainson's Hawk is the common buteo of the plains, a bird that is in many respects unique but at the same time seems to have traits drawn from a number of raptorial species. In a soar, the bird greatly resembles a Peregrine with its long, tapered wings, but when it is gliding, the wings are crooked like those of an Osprey. Swainson's hunts like a Harrier, migrates in large swirling flocks like a Broad-winged, and spends a good deal of time perched on the ground like the Ferruginous Hawk.

Immature Swainson's Hawk (*center*) with adult (*left*) and immature Broad-wingeds.

Swainson's is a bird of arid and semiarid regions. Its range extends into the Alaskan interior, but its stronghold is on the northern plains. It has the most arduous migration of any North American raptor. Birds entirely vacate breeding ranges in North America to winter in the pampas of Argentina. A small number of strays stay in southern Florida each winter.

Though the bird is a competent mouser, its chief prey is insects. It feeds heavily on grasshoppers and crickets and is commonly seen feeding on the ground, often in association with other Swainson's Hawks. At times, the bird hunts using the low, coursing flight of a Harrier, taking quicker prey by surprise.

The migration of Swainson's is as spectacular as that of the more heralded Broad-winged Hawk. Flocks numbering more than several thousand individuals have been recorded in southern Texas and, of course, in Panama, the bottleneck between the continents. In winter, the highly gregarious bird reportedly continues to show social habits.

Swainson's is a westerner and is likely to remain one, but the northern reach of its breeding range and the long-range nature of its migration (and the tendency of young birds to wander) mean stray birds reach the East Coast each autumn. In fact, Swainson's is an expected annual visitor at Cape May, New Jersey, and at Hawk Mountain, Pennsylvania.

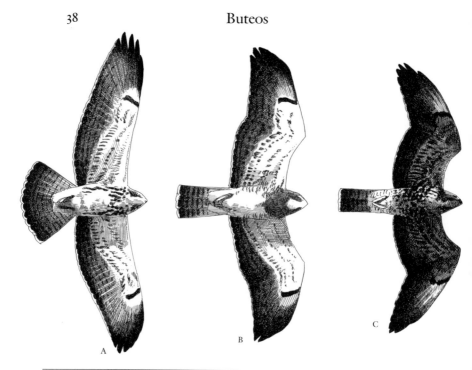

Swainson's Hawk, underside.
  (A) Immature
  (B) Adult
  (C) Immature
Slim, long-winged, and long-tailed. Wings smoothly curved and pointed;
gliding shape (B, C) is very distinctive. All plumages have dark flight feathers
that are darker toward tip, contrasting in light phase with paler coverts and
body. All show finely barred gray-brown tail and pale spot at base of outer
primaries adjacent to dark comma. Immatures are white to buffy below, with
streaking concentrated on breast and flanks; darker individuals (C) have
heavy black spotting across belly and on wing coverts. Adults vary, ranging
from typical light phase (B), with rusty brown breast band and fine barring
on flanks, to heavily barred rusty on entire underside to entirely blackish but
always with pale undertail coverts.

The origin of the eastern vagrants is unknown. It has been spec-
ulated that the birds are trapped on the north side of the Great
Lakes and travel east until they outdistance the water barrier.
Hawk Mountain and Cape May are almost due south of the eastern end of Lake Ontario.

A   B

Swainson's Hawk, upperside.
  (A) Adult
  (B) Immature
Both show faint pattern, for example on underside of light coverts, and
darker flight feathers; on some individuals this pattern is visible at a great
distance. Adult is smooth dark brown; immature has white rump band and
white spotting and edging on coverts and scapulars. Some immatures are
strikingly white-headed, particularly in spring and early summer when
feathers are worn.

IDENTIFICATION. Swainson's Hawk is a large, slim-winged, long-
tailed buteo with a mixed bag of raptor traits.

The backs of both adults and immatures are dark except for a
white patch on the basal portion of the tail — almost a rump
patch. Below, underwing linings and body are creamy to tawny-
colored. Adults have a dark chestnut bib that covers the chest but
leaves a white throat and face patch. Immatures mimic the adult's
pattern, with varying amounts of dark streaking on the underparts but particularly on the chest. Dark-phase Swainson's Hawks
are not uncommon.

In all plumages, the flight feathers are dark. On light-phase
birds they contrast noticeably with the lighter underwing coverts.

On dark-phase birds the entire underwing (and body) will look dark to black.

Immature birds occasionally show dark tones only on the trailing edge of the wing. Seen close up, the wing seems to have an ill-defined dark border. More commonly, though, the primaries and secondaries appear dark throughout, and the farther away the bird is, the darker the flight feathers seem to appear. The dark flight feathers and pale underwing linings are the best field marks.

During a full soar, the wings are long, narrow, and tapered like long candlesticks. They are usually thrust forward well ahead of the body. When the tail is fanned, the bird bears an uncanny resemblance to a soaring Peregrine Falcon. The wings are usually held in a pronounced dihedral, with the arms stiffly uplifted and the hands curved gently up. Swainson's is very buoyant in flight and rocks back and forth, like a tightrope walker trying to maintain his balance (also like a Turkey Vulture or a Harrier). A gliding Swainson's Hawk holds its wings in a unique configuration, and the bird glides a great deal. The glide configuration combines the bold dihedral of a Harrier and the crooked wings of an Osprey. The bird looks as if all of its weight were resting on its hands.

In low, hunting flight or head-on, Swainson's can look deceptively like a Harrier, but seen in silhouette from below, it is more suggestive of a thin and tapered-winged Rough-legged Hawk.

Rule of thumb: if you have a bird that you initially identify as a Harrier but that, as it approaches, takes on more and more the characteristics of a buteo, you are probably looking at a Swainson's Hawk.

Secondary field marks include heavy dark streaking on the chest and sides of the throat (immatures), a white patch at the base of the tail (nearly as pronounced as that on a Harrier), and a light area encircling the bill, in contrast with the dark head and face.

Rough-legged Hawk

This is a buteo of the high Arctic, feathered to the foot, hence its name. Most hawks have bare tarsi.

Unlike other North American buteos, the Rough-legged Hawk is not limited to the New World. Its distribution is circumpolar;

Adult Rough-legged Hawk (*left*) with adult Ferruginous (*right*).

arctic breeding populations may be found in North America, Greenland, Europe, and Asia. In North America, one subspecies, *B. l. sanctijohannis*, is native.

Like its arctic neighbors, the Gyrfalcon and the Peregrine, the Rough-legged is a cliff-nesting raptor. Often the three species will alternate at nest sites; the Gyr through usurpation (Gyrs nest earlier than Rough-leggeds) and the Peregrines through outright competition. The birds breed from the eastern Aleutians across coastal and arctic Alaska, the Northwest Territories, and northern Manitoba to northern Labrador, Newfoundland, and southeastern Quebec.

In winter, the bird stays for the most part south of Canada. Though it is largely absent in the Old South, large numbers winter in the Sun Belt. The Rough-legged's preferred hunting habitat is low, wet marsh, agricultural areas, and grasslands. A hunting Rough-legged will glide to an auspicious-looking site and hover, its head sweeping from side to side as the bird searches for its favorite prey, *Microtus* in winter and lemmings in summer. Small mammals constitute almost all of the diet. Avian prey is eaten only incidentally in both summer and winter.

If prey is sighted, the Rough-legged drops, legs extended; if the site is barren, the bird glides a short distance and hovers over the next likely stop. Most hunting is conducted at altitudes of 50–

100 feet, but it is not uncommon to find Rough-leggeds hovering at twice this altitude (and higher).

Fall migration begins in late September and lasts through the first week in December. Spring migration begins in late February in some locations, as birds adjust their winter territories to take advantage of early spring thaws, and starts in earnest in March; it continues into early May. There are few summer records of Rough-legged Hawks south of Canada.

The Rough-legged Hawk is one of the least common migrants at established eastern hawk-watch locations. Sites on the north side of the Great Lakes (particularly Lake Superior) offer the opportunity to see numbers of individuals as they make their way to key wintering areas in the plains and the Midwest. Derby Hill, in New York on the south shore of Lake Ontario, catches the rebound in the spring.

IDENTIFICATION. The Rough-legged Hawk is a large, lanky, angular buteo. It is boldly patterned, setting the bird apart from most buteos, with their subtle differences in plumage. Several different plumages occur, relating to age and sex, but these are blatant and readily separate light-phase birds from other species. Dark-phase Rough-leggeds have their own special problems, but in the East, a dark-phase buteo is *far* more likely to be a Rough-legged Hawk than any other species. In the West, the dark phase is uncommon, but in the East, at some migration count sites and on key wintering areas, dark-phase birds may be almost as numerous as light phase.

Light-phase Rough-leggeds have brown backs and a creamy or tawny crown and nape (usually overstreaked with brown). The upper surface of the tail is white except for a broad, dark band at the tip. Dark-phase birds show almost no white on the tail, and some have none at all.

On their underparts light-phase birds show four prominent field marks: two bold black or brown patches on the carpal joint of each wing; a heavy, thick swath of dark feathers right across the belly; and a wide dark band painted clear across the tip of the tail. These marks are most prominent on immature birds. Imma-

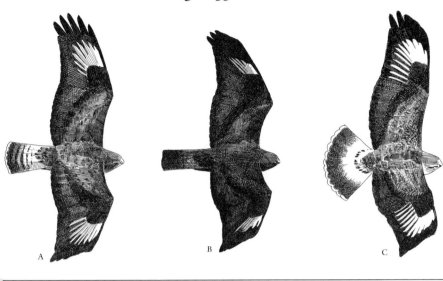

A   B   C

Rough-legged Hawk, upperside.
  (A) Typical adult
  (B) Dark extreme
  (C) Immature light extreme
All show light patch at base of at least outer primaries and have dark greater
coverts, contrasting with paler back and lesser coverts. Adults have barred
tails. Immatures probably have on average more white in primaries, but
variation is considerable and complex.

tures are largely unstreaked and very pale below. Adults are very
heavily streaked on the chest, making the belly band less conspicuous but the bird no less distinctive. Adult males have narrow
dark bands on the tail (in addition to the broad terminal band).
Females and immatures have clean, unmarked undertails (so that
the terminal band is even more prominent).

Dark-phase birds have black bodies and black underwing linings, which contrast with the very silvery white flight feathers and
undertail. In all but a few dark-plumaged birds, a broad, dark
subterminal band is obvious and diagnostic; in the East the bird
may be confused only with the immature Golden Eagle and Harlan's in the West.

The wings are very long and quite uniformly broad along their

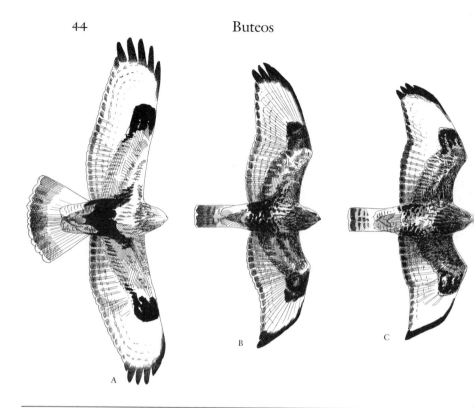

Rough-legged Hawk, underside.
  (A) Immature
  (B) Adult female
  (C) Adult male

Long-winged, lanky, and angular; long-tailed; head large and round. All plumages show blackish carpal patch and silvery flight feathers; most show blackish belly patch, but adult males typically have breast darker than belly (C). Immatures differ from adults in having little or no streaking or spotting below, solid blackish belly and carpal patches, and pale gray, not blackish, tips on primaries, secondaries, and tail feathers.

length. The lines are clean, trim, and nicely angled in a fashion that avoids any suggestion of stiffness. The hands are modestly tapered, adding a grace to the wing shape. The bird appears long-limbed but solid. The tail too is long and broad.

During a soar or a glide, the wings are held at a right angle to
the body. Head-on, the bird shows a very pronounced dihedral,
with wings that jut up sharply from the body and flatten out
at the wrist. Though many buteos fly with a dihedral, the Rough-
legged alone shows this up-and-out, hunched-shoulder configuration.

In point-to-point level flight, Rough-leggeds retain their long-
winged look, although the taper becomes acute. The wing beat is
steady. It does not frequently occur in a series, as with other buteos, but if the bird does fly in a series of pumps and glides, there
are more pumps to the glide.

The wing beats are unhurried, methodical, and deeply arched.
The flight seems effortless and is executed with a sense of purpose
— it is graceful, like a practiced movement.

Of all the members of the buteo clan, Rough-leggeds depend
least on thermals in migration. They readily use their own powers
of flight to travel from one place to another and no doubt for this
reason are the least hesitant of the buteos about crossing open
water. They are often the first buteo to appear in the morning
during a hawk watch and the last to be recorded in the afternoon.

Ferruginous Hawk

If the Ferruginous Hawk were an Old World raptor, it would
almost certainly be classed as an eagle (and more than one student
of raptors has argued for just such a reclassification). In both size
and reputation, the bird stands at least midway between the bu-

Immature Ferruginous Hawk in typical posture, perched on ground.

teos and the *Aquila* eagles. The largest buteo, it applies the hunting skills and techniques of a Golden Eagle.

The bird is a westerner, a bird of dry, open country — sage flats, shortgrass meadows, and desert. If political boundaries had figured more prominently in the selection of our national symbol, the Ferruginous Hawk would have been a prime candidate. Its breeding and wintering range is almost wholly confined to the continental United States.

Small mammals are the bird's preferred prey, especially ground squirrels and the several species of prairie dogs in particular. Jackrabbits, Prairie Chickens, Sage Grouse, and pheasants are not overlooked, particularly in winter, when hibernation puts favored prey species out of reach.

Adult Ferruginous Hawk gliding head-on.

The Ferruginous Hawk is an active hunter, hovering like a Rough-legged, kiting like a Red-tailed, and quartering high over the plains, with its wings raised and its head turned down as it studies each promising movement below.

During the warmer months, when ground squirrels are active, the birds frequently hunt by cruising low in the manner of the Golden Eagle, another hill-country hunter. The long, wide wings drawn in and tempered into hunting points, and the heavy, powerful, tireless wing beats and sweeping glides make a Ferruginous Hawk easy to mistake for an eagle.

Only Harriers like to spend as much time sitting on open ground as Ferruginous Hawks do. Other buteos seem out of place on flat, open terrain, but the Ferruginous Hawk's long, low profile, coupled with its alert, erect stance and elevated head, make it appear very much at home on the ground. The bird often selects a ground perch even when a suitable elevated perch is nearby.

The statement that the Ferruginous Hawk is migratory must be qualified. The bird does vacate northern portions of its range in colder months, and part of the population moves across the border into northern Mexico. For the most part, migrations are local. Birds move from their summer ranges (near prairie dog cities) and congregate in areas with a stable food supply during the hard months. Young birds range more widely than adults and have on occasion been recorded in such out-of-the-way places as Illinois, New Jersey, and Florida.

IDENTIFICATION. The Ferruginous Hawk is a very large, heavily structured buteo with a striking plumage and the demeanor of a hunting eagle. Its body is heavy and barrel-chested. The head is large, angular, and prominent, protruding from a heavy, snakelike neck.

Light-phase adults are a warm rufous on the back and shoulders. They often appear quite light at a distance, but dark spotting is evident at close range. Immatures lack the reddish cast. Dark-phase birds also occur.

The wings are gray-brown above, setting off two prominent white wing patches much like those of an immature Golden Eagle. These wing patches may appear as shafts of white on the upper surface of the wings or as large white blotches. The wing patches are more prominent on immatures, but in any plumage they are obvious and highly visible even at great distances.

The head is paler than the back but has a dark cap. Most birds appear dark-headed at a distance. The bird frequently glides and soars with its head turned downward.

The tail is long, very broad, usually closed, and never fanned as broadly as that of a soaring Red-tailed. It is, in all plumages, pale below with a dirty tip that is not distinctly banded. Seen from above, the tails range from a wash of pale brown to creamy white, which extends from one-half to two-thirds of the bird's length. The balance of the tail is reddish, the color being sometimes prominent and bright and sometimes no more than a wash near the tip. Immatures have narrow bands on the tails that are not visible at a distance.

Underparts (body, wings, and tail) are starkly *white* at a dis-

Ferruginous Hawk, underside.
  (A) Typical adult
  (B) Heavily marked adult
  (C) Immature
Large and long-winged with pointed wing tips; broad-armed and small-handed. Wings can appear very pointed in glide, especially on immature. Head and bill larger than on Rough-legged. Body normally strikingly white; dark birds such as the one shown in (B) are very uncommon. Underwing sparsely spotted; may show dark patagium but only when entire underwing is heavily marked (as in B); all have dark comma and silvery white flight feathers with little or no barring and pale gray tips. Adult has rusty blotching on underwing, rusty leggings, pale gray and rufous tail. Much variation between (A) and (B). Immature (C) has blackish spotting on underwing and lower flanks; gray, not black, tips on primaries; and faint barring on secondaries and tail.

tance (whiter than those of any other buteo except Krider's Red-tailed). Adults, and to a lesser extent immatures, have degrees of flecking or patterning on the sides of the chest and down the flanks, but the impression of utter whiteness is rarely diminished.

A

B

Ferruginous Hawk, upperside.
   (A) Adult
   (B) Immature
Adult is bright rusty on back and wing coverts. Flight feathers gray, with
white showing on inner webs of primaries; white at base of tail variable. Tail
generally looks gray-brown when closed and exposes white inner webs when
fanned; head varies from whitish to dark gray. Immature is brown with white
spotting and extensive white in primaries and secondaries. All ages show dark
greater coverts and pale base of primary coverts.

The reddish leggings of adult birds are very apparent and are diagnostic. Leggings will occasionally fuse into the semblance of a
belly band. Immatures may lack any spotting on the legs what-
soever.

   The clean white underwings set off the bold, black commas at
the wrist of each wing. These marks are prominent even on dark-
phase birds (which have reddish brown or charcoal brown wing
linings). The patagium on light-phase birds is usually pale; some
birds show a smudgy leading edge to the wing, but it is never as
dark as the patagium on a Red-tailed Hawk. The trailing edge of

the wing linings is usually darkly flecked, however, so that a line seems to be running down the middle of the wing. A few birds have very extensive flecking and patterning on the wing linings (the coloration suggests a middle grade between the light phase and the dark).

The wings are long, broad, and eaglelike. In a full soar, the lines are smooth, clean-edged and not bulging. The leading edge is straight cut; the trailing edge is gently rounded. The bird appears long-armed and small-handed and boasts the clean, symmetrical lines of a soft-nosed bullet. When the Ferruginous Hawk is soaring, the uplifted wings recall a Swainson's Hawk. When the bird is gliding or flying point to point, the primaries are closed and the wings draw back, so that they have a very pointy appearance, making the bird look like a buteo with the bearing of an eagle and the sympathies of a falcon.

To observers familiar with the Ferruginous Hawk, the silhouette and mannerisms make it as readily identifiable as a Peregrine at any distance imaginable. In any plumage, the Ferruginous Hawk will display three unmistakable points of light: one at each wing tip and one at the base of the tail (clearly the bird's best field mark).

The wing beat is more fluid than that of a Red-tailed, no doubt because of the bird's astounding wing length. In flight the bird appears somewhat like a heavily flapping Swainson's Hawk or a Harrier with the lumbering, almost mechanical grace of a Golden Eagle. Contrary to some accounts, the Ferruginous Hawk hovers frequently, with a style somewhat recalling that of a hovering Osprey — deep wing beats with a great deal of wrist movement.

Telling Buteos Apart

At first glance, buteos are technically easier to identify than falcons or accipiters because the observer relies strongly on a system of field marks made familiar by 50 years of Peterson plates. At the same time, however, the identification process is complicated by many variables. There are only three possible accipiters and only three or four possible falcons (depending on the locale), with five (the Gyrfalcon) an outside possibility. Where buteos are concerned, there are five front-line possibilities in most of North America even if we overlook for the moment birds that may or may not be subspecies.

Eliminate variables even before you start watching hawks. Observers at most points on the continent can eliminate one or two possibilities on the basis of range. Broad-winged Hawks are not very likely in Arizona. Rough-legged Hawks rarely reach Georgia. Swainson's Hawks would stop traffic in New Hampshire, and Ferruginous Hawks make very few appearances in Ohio (or in Pennsylvania, Maryland, Delaware, or Virginia).

It is also useful to heed migratory timetables. A distant buteo might well be a Broad-winged Hawk in September but probably not in late November.

Buteo identification can often be reduced to a choice between one or two realistic possibilities or may simply involve confirming or disaffirming the expected occurrence. If it is September 9 and you should be seeing Broad-winged Hawks, why not check for Broad-winged Hawk characteristics before straining to see windows, commas, or belly bands and starting from scratch.

Most buteos that are identified first appear as distant, soaring specks and gradually approach the watch point. Buteos in flocks are in most cases (and for the majority of hawk-watch locations) Broad-winged Hawks (eastern United States) or Swainson's Hawks (western United States) or both (Texas and vicinity). *Caution: there are other flocking raptors besides buteos (for example, Mississippi Kites and vultures), and other large birds migrate in flocks and soar (for example, cormorants and Sandhill Cranes).* Kettles of Red-taileds, Red-shouldereds, and even accipiters numbering 10 to more than 100 have occurred at some coastal hawk-watch sites and at locations in the Great Lakes, but these are exceptional.

When a bird is first viewed, at the limit of conjecture, only the most conspicuous field marks are visible — for example, the three points of light on a Ferruginous Hawk and the red tail on the adult Red-tailed Hawk.

Sometimes, a buteo's way of holding its wings offers a clue. Rough-leggeds hold their wings in a dihedral that juts upward abruptly from the shoulders and flattens out along its length;

Red-taileds have a dihedral that starts flat and lifts upward toward the tip. When Swainson's is gliding, its hands drop down like an Osprey's wing. Broad-wingeds soar on flat wings, and Red-shouldered Hawks usually hold their wings slightly drooped, cupping the wind.

Motion, the rhythm and pattern of flight, is evident long before plumage characteristics may be noted. Study the wing beats. A Ferruginous Hawk will have slow, pushing, fluid wing beats that suggest an eagle. A Red-tailed Hawk will have a quicker, heavy series of wing beats that seem to roll down the wing. Swainson's Hawks have stiff, languid, downward-pushing wing beats. Rough-leggeds have deep, arcing, purposeful wing beats that are often continuous (and are only rarely interrupted by a glide). Red-shouldereds have quick, accipiterlike wing beats that are stiff at the shoulder and loose at the wrist; they seem to bat the air. Broad-wingeds have a quick, stiff, choppy wing beat that occurs in a series and is frequent.

Finally, as the bird approaches and you begin to see key plumage points, mark the streakings, the tail band(s), the windows, and the patagium — the marks that clinch the shoestring calls (or contradict them).

Accipiters
The Artful Dodgers

SPECIES

Sharp-shinned Hawk, *Accipiter striatus*
Cooper's Hawk, *A. cooperi*
Northern Goshawk, *A. gentilis*

The accipiters are quick, agile raptors of boreal forest, bayberry thicket, and backyard bird feeder. These are bird-catching hawks, "true hawks," in the meaning of the Latin word *Accipiter*. Evolution's push and pull has created here a group of birds designed to capture other birds in deep woods and thick growth. An accipiter's wings are typically short and rounded, adapted for bursts of weaving flight through heavy brush on a path that a falcon or a buteo cannot follow. If a Cooper's Hawk is released in front of a seemingly impenetrable maze of branches, the bird will melt away with no more than a vibrating twig or two to mark its entry point.

The hair-trigger reflexes and long, rudderlike tail permit the Sharp-shinned Hawk and Cooper's Hawk to follow the twisting, turning escape flight of passerine prey. Goshawks simply bear down on larger prey in a short, weaving, one-sided dash.

Accipiters are not like falcons, which make light of distances; the true hawk is a sprinter. If prey is not taken in the first attempt or after a short chase, pursuit is broken off. Surprise is the ally of an accipiter, not endurance.

Three species of the genus *Accipiter* occur in North America. In order of relative abundance (over most of their range) these are the Sharp-shinned Hawk, Cooper's Hawk, and the Goshawk.

Migration

Sharp-shinned Hawks and Cooper's Hawks are migratory in the classic sense. Most members of the populations move south be-

Accipiters: soaring immatures of all species. Males are shown; females are significantly larger in all species but do not overlap other species (female Sharp-shinned is nearly as large as male Cooper's; female Cooper's nearly as large as male Goshawk and as large as Broad-winged; female Goshawk as large as some Red-taileds). Adults of all species are shorter-tailed, and longer-winged than immatures.

(A) Sharp-shinned Hawk: short broad wings that are pushed forward in soar, all edges curved; head small; wing tips often thrust forward of head; tail with square corners. Body and underwing coverts heavily streaked; narrow gray tip on tail.

(B) Cooper's Hawk: longer wings, head, and tail; tubular body. Wings are held straight in soar, with straighter edges and narrower tips than on Sharp-shinned; head is long; tail long and rounded. The body and underwing coverts are white with fine streaking, contrasting with the darker, orange-brown head; tail has a bold white tip.

(C) Northern Goshawk: long wings, very broad in the secondaries and narrow at the tip; broad, heavy body and head; and broad tail. Body and underwing coverts are dingy white with heavy streaking. Flight feathers may appear darker than underwing coverts.

fore the leaves have left the trees, following a timetable which corresponds to the migration schedule of their passerine prey. Birds which have hatched that year precede adults. Fall migration for Sharp-shinneds begins during the first week in September, peaks later that month or during the first week in October, and continues into mid-November. Spring migration occurs largely in April; it peaks late in the month or during the first few days in May and falls off quickly, to be completed before midmonth.

Cooper's Hawk migration runs about two weeks later than Sharp-shinned migration in the fall and peaks two weeks earlier in the spring. Adults and immatures of both species appear to favor different migration routes. Immature accipiters constitute almost 95 percent of the coastal accipiter flight; adult birds account for more than three-quarters of the flight witnessed at interior lookouts.

Goshawk migration is less an annual event than a cyclic occurrence prompted by the abundance of prey. During years when Ruffed Grouse and snowshoe hare are plentiful, Goshawks do not move south in large numbers, and those that are seen are usually hatching-year birds. During years when both species of prey are at a low point in their population cycles (about once every decade), large numbers of adult birds move south, marking what is called an invasion year. An invasion occurred in 1972 over much of North America. Another occurred in 1982, but its scope was limited to the west side of the Great Lakes.

Accipiter migration is largely a morning phenomenon. On major flights, birds are moving before sunrise. As the afternoon progresses, birds devote more attention to securing prey than to covering ground.

Identification

Distinguishing one accipiter from another is *not* easy. It is, in fact, one of the most difficult identification problems facing hawk watchers. Even veteran observers do not always agree. Arguments about identification of accipiters may well account for more broken friendships and more failed marriages between hawk watchers than all other causes combined.

All three accipiters have roughly similar shapes, with short, round wings and a long, narrow tail. Immature birds have almost identical plumages. Of the adults, only the Goshawk is distinctly different. The plumages of adult Sharp-shinned and Cooper's hawks are virtually the same.

All three species are separable by size, but size alone is of limited value in the field, where the tool in hand is a pair of binoculars, not a wing-chord meter. Attempts to distinguish the species by size are complicated by two other factors. First, size varies greatly between males and females within species. Female accipiters are about one-third larger than their male counterparts. Second, adults and immatures have different proportions. Immatures have shorter and broader wings and longer tails than adults (in other words, immatures have a different shape).

The extreme variability of course contributes greatly to the confusion of hawk watchers. The differences in size *within* each species offer little basis for distinctions *between* species. Not only do female Sharp-shinned Hawks approach male Cooper's Hawks in size, but adult Cooper's Hawks approach immature Sharp-shinned Hawks in shape! The shorter tail of an adult Cooper's Hawk (coupled with the longer wings, which make the head and tail appear even shorter) gives the bird a stocky appearance more commonly associated with the Sharp-shinned Hawk.

Difficulties notwithstanding, identification of accipiters is not the impossible feat that some observers have made it seem. A number of clues (and a few blatant field marks), taken together, make possible accurate identifications. *Don't rely on just one or two field marks.* Use many. And remember, no one can be right all of the time, and no one who has watched hawks for any length of time expects to be.

Accipiter identification is tough and challenging. It gives hawk watchers the chance to earn their spurs. When you can honestly say that you feel comfortable telling Sharp-shinned Hawks apart from Cooper's Hawks, you can call yourself an expert among hawk watchers.

The balance of this section on accipiter identification will focus on immature birds in discussing plumage, for several reasons. First, the difference between an adult Goshawk, with its blue-gray back and pale gray underparts, and the adult Cooper's and Sharp-shinned hawks, with their dark, slaty-blue upperparts and orange breast, is extreme and obvious.

Second, plumage differences between adult Sharp-shinned Hawks and adult Cooper's Hawks are virtually nonexistent. One salient feature, the width of the terminal band on the tail, also occurs on immatures. The other, a contrasting dark cap found on the head of Cooper's Hawks but not on Sharp-shinneds, is not very apparent in the field (and would complicate an already difficult chapter if we included it here).

Finally, accipiter identification is largely a matter of shapes, relative proportions, and manner of flight, and these subjects can be discussed without reference to plumage.

The Generic Accipiter

The accipiter is usually a short, broad, and round-winged raptor with a long, narrow tail. The size varies considerably. The bird is brown above and creamy below, with streaked underparts. The tail is banded. The bird has an eyestripe and white undertail coverts. It generally flies with a series of flaps interspersed with a glide. The tail is usually folded. The accipiter uses thermals for lift and, when soaring, fans its tail.

Sharp-shinned Hawk

The Sharp-shinned Hawk is a small, scrappy, compact raptor. As a breeding species, migrant, or wintering bird, it occurs throughout North America south of the tundra. Except in the American West, where the larger Cooper's Hawk has a numerical edge, it is by far the most common accipiter to be seen during migration.

Anything that wears feathers and is in the bantamweight class is eligible as prey for the Sharp-shinned Hawk. Although the hawks have taken prey as large as Common Flickers, they usually prefer passerines the size of warblers and finches.

In the hunting mode, the Sharp-shinned maneuvers deftly through woodlands, following the contours of hedgerows and moving quickly in and out of breaks in the foliage as it searches

Sharp-shinned Hawks.

Sharp-shinned Hawk stooping.

Adult male Sharp-shinned Hawk.

for prey. Its chief weapons are surprise, rapid acceleration, and reflexes so quick that a Sharp-shinned Hawk's movements seem not just to mirror the escape tactics of prey but to anticipate them. If prey is not secured after a brief, acrobatic chase, however, pursuit ends quickly. The long, spirited, winding chases through brush and bramble are a myth.

Each fall at Cape May, New Jersey (a location that more Sharp-shinned Hawks pass in a season's migration than most hawk-watch sites see in 10), tokens of successful hunts carpet the ground. After a major flight in late September or early October, the woodland floor is littered with rings of feathers that are soon scattered by the wind.

In winter, the Sharp-shinned Hawk often stakes a claim to one or more backyard feeding stations. Many a bird enthusiast has wondered why the White-throated Sparrows on the window tray suddenly froze, nor is it uncommon to see the small blue hawk in action, pinning backyard prey to the ground. Nature centers continue to receive calls from hysterical homeowners, demanding that something be done about the murdering creature, but as more people begin to understand and accept predators in their established role , the Sharp-shinned Hawk becomes another bird as visitor to watch for.

Suburban feeding stations are dangerous for Sharp-shinned Hawks (and for other species). Plate glass doors and picture windows are the major cause of Sharp-shinned mortality reported to the Bird Banding Laboratory. The surface of glass reflects the image of surrounding bushes and trees; knowing nothing about reflecting surfaces, a flying raptor and a fleeing junco may see nothing but more woods. The accipiter too often suffers a concussion or a broken neck, and the homeowner may have a broken window.

On its territory, the bird is secretive. Nests are well hidden, high in a spruce or other conifer. Caution is the hallmark of the Sharp-shinned Hawk. Although it is a raptor, it is not exempt from predation. In fact, its size makes it exceptionally vulnerable to larger species of raptors, including Cooper's Hawks, Harriers, Red-tailed Hawks, and Peregrine Falcons.

In migration, the bird is as much at home on the interior ridges as it is on the coast. Sharp-shinneds frequently travel in pairs or in groups of three, four, five, or more birds.

IDENTIFICATION. This raptor is somewhere in size between a robin and a pigeon. Males are smaller than females. Overall, the

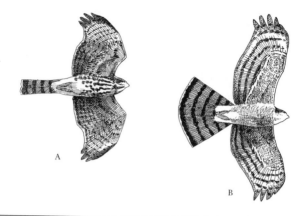

Sharp-shinned Hawk, underside.
(A) Immature
(B) Adult
Wings always pushed forward, with distinct S-curve on trailing edge; tail narrow and square-tipped; wings and tail average slightly longer on immature. Immature heavily streaked and spotted on body and underwing coverts, appearing dirty brown and lacking pale underwing coverts and the contrast between head and body evident on Cooper's. Adult plumage identical to Cooper's except for narrower pale tip on tail.

Sharp-shinned Hawk represents the stubby, chunky extreme of the accipiter line. The tail is long and narrow, in classic accipiter fashion, but even the larger female appears stocky rather than long or rangy.

The wings are short, quite rounded at the tip, and very broad. The trailing edge is sharply curved in an S-shape — a broad arm arcing into a small hand. On the leading edge of the wing, the wrist juts abruptly forward, so that the bird has a hunched appearance.

The body is slight. Soaring high overhead, the Sharp-shinned Hawk appears to be nothing but wing and tail: a flying mallet. The tail is usually notched or square-tipped, but some individuals, for assorted reasons, have tails that are slightly rounded. Rare individuals have a very round tip to the tail, but the tip is never spatula-shaped or knobbed but simply rounded.

Thick and noodlelike streaking on the underparts extends from the chest down to the belly. At a distance, the underparts look

Sharp-shinned Hawk, upperside.
   (A) Adult male
   (B) Immature female
Adult is blue-gray with blackish wing tips and tail bands, palest on rump;
immature is uniform dark brown above, with irregular white spotting on
back. Other immature accipiters have buffy spotting on back and are paler
and more patterned. Adult is distinguishable from Cooper's by narrow gray
tail tip and cap, which is not noticeably darker than back; adult females are
duller and browner above than males, and so adults might be sexed by color.
A bird of known sex is more easily identified by size.

dirty. The tail is banded alternately light and dark. The tip (or
terminal band) is narrow, not sharply defined, and dirty gray, not
white.

   In soaring flight, the wings are generally held flat out to the
sides or gently droop down. In a partial tuck, when the bird is
riding the updraft off a ridge, the wings may be angled downward. The tail will be cocked upward.

   The small size of the Sharp-shinned means a rapid wing beat.
The flaps are quick, snappy, hurried, and too rapid to count. Each
series of wing beats is punctuated by a glide.

   Sharp-shinned Hawks frequently travel in pairs or in small
groups (with as many as eight individuals). They are feisty and
frequently harass other raptors as large as or larger than themselves (including other Sharp-shinned Hawks) during migration.

Cooper's Hawk

If you took a Sharp-shinned Hawk, grabbed its head and tail and
gave a steady pull, and then did the same things to the wings,
you'd have a bird that bore some resemblance to a Cooper's

Immature Cooper's (*right*) soaring with two Sharp-shinneds.

Hawk, but chances are that it would still fall short of expectations. Cooper's Hawk is a larger southern cousin of the Sharp-shinned Hawk. The differences in plumage between the two are so subtle that differentiating them has become a standard of achievement in hawk-watching circles.

The Cooper's Hawk is at home in the deciduous woodlands of North Carolina; in the hilltop, hardwood strongholds of Ohio; in the riverbottom cottonwoods of Colorado; and on the forested slopes of California's coast. Its range falls almost entirely within the borders of the continental United States. This territory, along with its former abundance and preference for prey larger than that taken by the Sharp-shinned Hawk, made the bird's conflicts with the continent's European invaders inevitable.

The colonists brought with them three things that had a direct and lasting impact on North America's medium-sized accipiter. First, they brought chickens. These slow-moving, dim-witted creatures have had much of the sense of survival bred out of them

Immature Sharp-shinned (*left*) and Cooper's Hawks, gliding.

with the passage of time. As luck would have it, the runty pro-
totypes of today's Oven Stuffer roasters were acceptable prey for
the Cooper's Hawk.

Second, Europe's religious, freedom-seeking people brought
with them the Bible, which gave them dominion over all the creatures of the earth.

Third, they carried under the crook of the arm a marvelous
instrument known as a muzzle-loader. Cooper's Hawks, of
course, could not distinguish between stupid chickens and infirm
Passenger Pigeons, and frontier farmers, whose resources were
sparse enough anyway, were equally unlikely to ignore the indis-
cretions of the hungry hawks.

There were other strikes against the bird, however. The pioneer
farmers soon learned that local game (and the word "game" covered a lot more ground than it does today, including robins and
flickers) could be hunted to fill plates on the dinner table. That
Cooper's Hawks felt the same way made no difference; nobody
likes competition.

Finally, the ornithologists of the day, needing a scapegoat in
their efforts to protect other raptors, pronounced the Cooper's
Hawk a worthy candidate for extermination. Condemnation of
the bird persisted even among ornithologists until well into the
twentieth century. Possibly our more enlightened attitude today
stems not from a better understanding of the role of predators
but from a reliance on the supermarket shelf as a source of chickens rather than the backyard henhouse.

IDENTIFICATION. Cooper's Hawk, a crow-sized raptor always
larger than a Sharp-shinned Hawk, is a long, lean, lanky accipiter.
The body is tube-shaped, heavier than that of a Sharp-shinned.
The tail is disproportionately long. The head is large and heavy
and protrudes well ahead of the wing (imagine a turtle extending
its head fully).

The wings are moderately long and cleanly tapered, lacking any
bumps or bulges. The even tapering often makes them appear
longer than they actually are. The leading edge is straight cut at a
right angle to the body, with little or no bend at the wrist. The

Cooper's Hawk, underside.
  (A) Immature
  (B) Adult
Long, tubular body; long head; wings fairly long and straight-edged; tail
long, club-shaped, rounded, tending toward wedge-shaped in females.
Immatures are slightly longer-tailed and longer- and thinner-winged than
adults. Adult has fine orange barring on body and underwing coverts.
Immature has white body and underwing coverts, with fine dark streaking
restricted to forward half of body, head solid orange-brown, contrasting
darkly with breast, underparts appear white at a distance, thereby differing
from those of both other accipiters. All ages have broad white tip on tail.

longer head and tail and longer wings give Cooper's Hawk the
shape of a flying cross.

Cooper's Hawks almost always have a very round tail. It is
sometimes cleanly and evenly convex, and it sometimes flares outward like a spoon. Sometimes, too, it is clover-shaped, with three
distinct lobes, but it is almost invariably *round*. Perhaps 1 in 80
Cooper's Hawks will have a tail that seems slightly square. Not
infrequently, birds with obviously rounded tails will show a slight
notch — but not the unmistakable dent that is visible in the tail
of many Sharp-shinned Hawks.

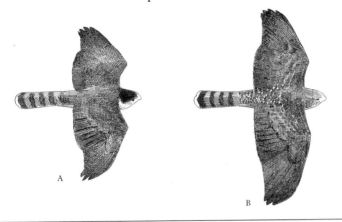

Cooper's Hawk, upperside.
   (A) Adult male
   (B) Immature female
Adult differs from Sharp-shinned only in broader whiter tip on tail and dark cap; females are browner above, less blue, and have less contrasting cap. Immature is brown with fine buffy spotting and edging, especially on lower back and rump, appearing paler, warmer, and less uniform than Sharp-shinned; tawny head can also be obvious from above.

   The tip of the tail has a broad white (not gray or dirty white) terminal band. This band is easily seen from above and is particularly obvious from below when the bird fans its tail in a full soar. The streaking on the underparts of an immature Cooper's Hawk is neat and fine and is restricted to the chest. At a distance, the underparts of an immature Cooper's Hawk appear clean and white (the streaking disappears).

   The wing beat of Cooper's is slower than that of a Sharp-shinned Hawk because the bird is larger. Movement is stiff and seems to be limited to the inner part of the wing. The bird flaps as though it were arthritic.

   Cooper's Hawks tend to be solitary birds. They are not wont to travel in pairs or small groups, and they are generally much less common than Sharp-shinneds during migration.

Adult Northern Goshawk.

Northern Goshawk

The Goshawk is a large, reticent raptor of northern forests. It has the size and power of a buteo and the killing skills of an accipiter. The bird's hunting prowess has given it a special place in the hearts of falconers. In the eyes of the hawk-watch community it is the equal of the Peregrine as "a bird to be seen."

The adult is as striking and beautiful as it is powerful — a shadow cast in gray, with piercing red eyes that radiate malevolence. The gray ghost runs down its classic prey, snowshoe hare and Ruffed Grouse, in an all-out aerial sprint. Goshawks exhibit a legendary single-mindedness with regard to prey. Accounts of hares pursued by Goshawks on the ground and through tangled thickets are common. Bent, in his *Life Histories of North American Birds of Prey,* tells the story of a Goshawk that pursued a chicken under the skirts of a farm wife, who sought to defend the fowl with a broom.

When a Goshawk binds to prey, it doesn't wait for constriction before claiming its victim. It foots repeatedly, seeking vital organs, as long as motion persists. In the north, in winter, prey is scarce. Something that moves lives. Something that lives may escape but not from a Goshawk.

The prowess of the bird is legendary, and as with most legends, the human mind has exceeded the limits of fact. On the Kittatinny Ridge one of the authors saw a yearling White-tailed Deer run across a clearing and stop at the crest of the ridge. The wind was in the man's favor; the deer didn't move. From the corner of his eye, he caught a hint of movement, then saw an adult female Goshawk closing the distance between them, flat out. In the confines of the small clearing, she appeared massive. The man's first reaction was, "My God! She is going to take the deer!" She didn't. The bird passed over the back of the stationary animal and instead took an immature Sharp-shinned Hawk migrating downridge.

Although Goshawks are most often regarded as a bird of deep northern pines, they are increasing in the deciduous woodlands of the Northeast — perhaps in response to the maturation of protected forests, perhaps filling the vacuum left by the declining Cooper's Hawk. In some places, the bird has become a suburban dweller, nesting in well-vegetated neighborhoods, becoming the terror of golden retrievers and of homeowners who set out trashcans on the curb. Maternal instincts run high in female Goshawks. They show little tolerance for any close approach to a nest site.

The size of the northern population is governed by the availability of prey, and it undergoes cycles of gradual increase and rapid decline. During years of scarcity, even the adult Goshawks move south, in what is called an "invasion." Then, along the ridges, the lake shores, and the coast, hawk watchers can watch the gray ghosts flow south.

IDENTIFICATION. The Goshawk is a large, buteo-sized, and buteo-shaped accipiter. The body is heavy but not chesty, with a moderately long but very broad tail. The tail itself barely deserves the name. It looks more like an extension of the body trailing out behind the wing. One observer has described the bird as a flying stovepipe.

Most Goshawks have an arcing tip to the tail, but wide variation in both tail shape and overall length is a hallmark of this bird. There are crop-tailed Goshawks and long-tailed Goshawks. Some have round-tipped tails, and others have square-cut tails. But variability notwithstanding, the tail on a Goshawk is always *broad.*

Northern Goshawk, underside.
  (A) Adult
  (B) Immature
Large and heavy, with big, tubular body; large, buteo-like head and broad tail
(shape of tail varies). Wings pinched at base, broad in secondaries and
narrower at tip; leading edge fairly straight, but S-curve on trailing edge may
recall Sharp-shinned. Immatures slightly longer-tailed and longer- and
thinner-winged than adults. Adult is easily separated from other accipiters by
pale gray barring on underparts and black eye patch. Immature differs from
Cooper's in having dingy brown body and underwing coverts with heavy
dark streaking and gray-brown, not orange, head. Differentiated from Sharp-
shinned by size; by dingy (not white) ground color on underparts; by lack of
blotchy bars on flanks; and by white tip on tail.

The wings are broad, too: broad, long, and severely tapered
toward the tip. The bird takes the wide-armed, small-handed
shape familiar from the wing of a Sharp-shinned Hawk, softens
it with the fluid lines of a Gyrfalcon, and adds the length of a
buteo. The Goshawk's head is large, broad, and shaped more like
a balled fist than like the head of a curious turtle. The eyeline is
usually pronounced.

Northern Goshawk, upperside.
  (A) Immature
  (B) Adult
Adult is varying shades of blue-gray with black cap; black-and-white head pattern is unique and distinctive. Back and wing coverts on immature are distinctly spotted; all feathers edged dull buff; white eyeline may appear on other accipiters.

The streaking on the breast is heavy and thick. The chest appears dirty or dark at a distance. The underwing is two-toned. Coverts appear light, whereas the flight feathers are in the shade. Undertail coverts are white with darker streaking, not gleaming white or fluffy. Immature birds vary in terms of the color or tone of their plumage. Some birds have a tan, gray, brown, or even purple cast.

The wing beat is heavy, deep, and labored like that of a buteo. When the bird is hunting or flying point to point, the wings become sharply tapered and are swept back like those of a falcon. This characteristic, in combination with the heavy body and long, broad tail, makes the Goshawk easy to confuse with a Gyrfalcon.

In a soar, with tail fanned and wings extended, however, the bird takes on the Gestalt of a buteo — more specifically, that of an immature Red-shouldered Hawk. *Rule of thumb: any bird that is first identified as a buteo and turns out to be an accipiter may safely be called a Goshawk.*

Telling Accipiters Apart

When an accipiter is spotted through the binoculars, the first thing to determine is its size. Is it big? Or is it small?

If the bird appears small right at the onset, it probably *is* small — a Sharp-shinned Hawk. Resist the temptation to make the bird larger than it really is.

But if the bird looks *big,* you need to decide *how* big. As big as a female Sharp-shinned or a male Cooper's Hawk? Or as big as a Goshawk? Accipiter identification is usually a matter of asking one of these two questions.

It is not as difficult to differentiate Sharp-shinned Hawks from Goshawks because the two species differ greatly in size. It is very fortunate that they do. If Sharp-shinned Hawks were the size of Cooper's Hawks, distinguishing between them and Goshawks would border on the impossible. In terms of shape and plumage, the two species are very similar (more similar to each other than to a Cooper's Hawk). The wing shape is nearly identical, in relative length their heads are comparable, and the chests of both are streaked and dirty. A high, soaring Goshawk is very likely to be mistaken for a Sharp-shinned Hawk — until it flaps. There is a world of difference between the snappy wing beat of a Sharpie and the deep, steady, rowing wing beat of a Goshawk.

SHARP-SHINNED VERSUS COOPER'S. Most observers look for one of two field marks to distinguish Sharp-shinneds from Cooper's: (1) the size and shape of the head and (2) the shape of the tip of the tail. Both marks are good indicators, but neither is infallible. No field mark is. Do not rely on just one or two features when you make identifications. Use a number of clues, and your chances of correctly identifying the bird will increase.

Of the two standard field marks, tail shape is less reliable. Accipiter tails show a fair degree of variability, although Sharp-shinneds can usually be counted upon to have square-cut or V-notched tails, and Cooper's Hawks almost always have well-rounded tails. But tail shape is affected by molt and feather wear. A tail that is partially fanned looks different from one that is fully closed. Even a slight degree of fallibility undermines confidence in a field mark. Identifications are second-guessed. Uncertainty creeps in. Then confusion. Then frustration.

Not that tail shape is not a good aid to accipiter identification or that a largish accipiter boasting a tail that is shaped like a tennis racket isn't a Cooper's Hawk. It almost certainly *is* a Cooper's Hawk, but you should look for a few other things just in passing.

If the bird is Cooper's, the head is bulky and protrudes well ahead of the wings, and the wings are straight along the leading edge. If the head is small and narrow and the wings jut forward at the wrist, the bird is more likely to be a Sharp-shinned Hawk.

A behavioral observation will also help. A passing raptor will notice a group of people standing on a mountaintop all looking its way. An accipiter that must drop a shoulder or turn its body to study the crowd is a Sharp-shinned Hawk. A Cooper's Hawk simply swivels its head, like a turtle looking back over its shell. The body stays firm.

If the tail is deeply notched or square, the bird is probably Sharp-shinned; if the tail is round, it might be Sharp-shinned. About 1 in every 10 Sharp-shinned Hawks has rounded corners on an otherwise square-cut tail. About 1 in 100 has a noticeably rounded tail.

Most Cooper's Hawks have very rounded tails, but you will occasionally find a square-tailed Cooper's Hawk. While you are looking at the tip of the tail, notice the light terminal band. If the band is narrow, ill defined, and off white, the bird is probably Sharp-shinned; if it is broad, sharply defined, and white, the bird may safely be identified as a Cooper's Hawk. This mark is visible from above, but it is particularly clear when the bird is backlit by the sun or is soaring with its tail fanned. One word of caution, though. Goshawks also have a white terminal band.

Although there is a great deal of variation, Cooper's Hawks appear to have longer tails than the average Sharp-shinned Hawk. Whether this is actually the case or is an illusion caused by the relative proportions of wing and tail is not important; field identification is concerned not with how things *are* but with how things *appear.*

In terms of overall Gestalt — the flash impression that veteran hawk watchers gain from hours spent studying head shape, wing length, tail length, and how these features interact — Sharp-shinneds are stocky accipiters; Cooper's Hawks appear lanky.

One or two other traits may usefully be considered. The thick, noodlelike streaking on the underparts of immature Sharp-shinned Hawks make the bird look dirty below. The neat, fine streaking on the chest of an immature Cooper's Hawk is invisible at a distance; its underparts look clean and white. *Rule of thumb: if an immature accipiter appears white below, it can safely be called a Cooper's.* Note that this mark applies only to the immature (brown-backed) birds. Adult Sharp-shinneds and Cooper's are barred with orange below, and given distance and bright sunlight, *both* species may show light underparts.

The pale underparts of an immature Cooper's Hawk contrast with and accentuate the bird's dark brown head. As a result, Cooper's Hawks appear to be wearing a hangman's hood.

Wing-on, when a Sharp-shinned Hawk heads downridge on set wings, riding the updraft, its tail cocks up at an angle. Cooper's Hawks in this attitude hold their tails horizontal. (American Kestrels hold their tails horizontal, too. Kestrels and Sharp-shinneds are about the same size and, when riding an updraft, may sometimes be confused.)

For the veteran hawk watcher, the clinching characteristic when a bird might be a Sharp-shinned Hawk or a Cooper's is the manner of flight. If the bird has a quick, snappy wing beat, it is Sharp-shinned. If the wing beat is slower and stiffer, with the motion centered at the arm and shoulder, the bird is Cooper's. Because Sharp-shinned Hawks weigh less, they bounce a good deal more when riding the updraft off a ridge. Cooper's Hawks look steadier.

Finally, it is far easier to identify a Sharp-shinned Hawk as Cooper's than to do the reverse. Cooper's Hawk really looks the part. The difficult cases usually involve Sharp-shinned Hawks with one or two borderline characteristics of Cooper's Hawk. If you really can't decide which bird it was, it was a Sharp-shinned Hawk.

COOPER'S VERSUS GOSHAWK. Sharp-shinned Hawks and Cooper's Hawks do not overlap in size, nor do Cooper's Hawks and Goshawks — in overall length, in wing length, or in weight. The largest female Cooper's Hawk will always be uncontestably smaller than the smallest male Goshawk. Nevertheless, distance diminishes dissimilarity. A difference of two or three inches isn't conspicuous at 300 yards. And if size alone were sufficient for accipiter identification, then the issue wouldn't be so controversial.

A quick, two-step process can effectively differentiate Cooper's Hawks from Goshawks. *Step 1: is the bird adult or immature?* An adult Goshawk with its pale blue-gray upperparts and light gray underparts — and also with a black cap, white eyeline, and dark facial patch — is about as different from the slate-blue, orange-breasted adult Cooper's Hawk as would be possible in nature.

If the bird is immature (if it is brown-backed, with streaked underparts), however, go to step 2. *Step 2: are the underparts heavily streaked (dirty), or are the underparts faintly streaked (clean and white)?* If the chest appears dirty at a distance, the bird is a Goshawk. If the underparts are pale white, it's Cooper's.

If the underparts are not visible (or if you prefer to play it safe), there are other distinguishing characteristics to note. The head on

Immature Cooper's Hawk (*left*) and Northern Goshawk (*right*).

Immature Red-shouldered (*right*) and Northern Goshawk (*left*).

a Cooper's Hawk is heavy and long, suggesting the head of a curious turtle. The head on a Goshawk appears squat and broad (more like that of a buteo than that of an accipiter).

The tail of a Goshawk is likewise very wide. It looks less like a tail than like a tube-shaped extension of the body. The tail on a Cooper's Hawk appears longer and narrower than the body. It *looks* like a tail.

The wings on a Goshawk are short and wide at the arm and narrow and long at the hand, with elements of the S-shaped curve seen on the wing of a Sharp-shinned Hawk. The Cooper's Hawk has a narrow, trim wing tapered slightly but evenly along its length.

In Gestalt a Cooper's Hawk is long, lean, and lanky; a Goshawk is heavy, broad, and buteo-like. The wing beat on a Goshawk is deep, heavy, and powerful. The wing beat of a Cooper's Hawk is stiff and shallow.

There are two other plumage characteristics. On many Goshawks, the underwings appear two-toned. The underwing linings are light, and the flight feathers appear darker, shaded. The underwing on a Cooper's Hawk is uniformly colored.

Finally, the streaking on the underparts of a Goshawk makes the chest appear dirty when it is viewed from a distance. But at close range, the spotting and streaking create a checkerboard pattern not seen on any other raptor.

In addition to features you *should* look for, there are a few traditional field marks that you should *not* look for, because either they don't work or they are wrong.

One example is fluffy white undertail coverts on a Goshawk. Adult Goshawks do indeed have them (in the breeding season), but they may be stained. There are much better marks on adult Goshawks, however, and the undertail coverts on immature Goshawks are actually more spotted than those found on Sharp-shinned Hawks or on Cooper's.

Another example is the bold white eyestripe on a Goshawk. Again, the adult has it and an adult Cooper's does not, but all immature accipiters have an eyestripe. The difference is a matter of degree. Our advice is not to rely on eyestripes to differentiate accipiters (and don't waste time looking for one when there are plenty of more substantive field marks to note).

Still another example is the zigzag or W-shaped barring on the tail of immature Goshawks. The pattern is real enough (even if it isn't obvious in the field), but some Cooper's Hawks have it, too. If you are close enough to see a zigzag pattern, why not just count the tail bands? Goshawks show four, Cooper's only three.

Falcons
Distance Measured by the Horizon

S P E C I E S

American Kestrel, *Falco sparverius*
Merlin, *F. columbarius*
Peregrine Falcon, *F. peregrinus*
Prairie Falcon, *F. mexicanus*
Gyrfalcon, *F. rusticolus*

An introduction to any bird bearing the name "falcon" seems unnecessary. Even a person who has never seen one knows that a falcon is a very fast hawk. Falcons are blade-winged sentinels standing guard in places where distances are measured by the horizon. These birds are at home on arctic tundra, prairie sage, floodplain, tidal flat, open marsh, plowed field, barrier beach, and, during migration, offshore waters — wherever the route between points A and B is a straight line.

A falcon is a mechanism of muscle and feathers designed to capture prey in flight. Accipiters are bushwhackers, masters of the artful dodge, with hair-trigger reflexes and agility that allows them to weave between branches. Falcons prefer wide open spaces; their mode of hunting is a one-on-one shootout, with all the chips going to the better flier.

Still, not all prey taken by falcons is airborne or, for that matter, capable of flight. The American Kestrel is a champion mouser, and ground squirrels are dietary mainstays for the Prairie Falcon. But these are exceptions to the general rule.

Of the North American falcons, only four can be classed as long-distance migrants: the American Kestrel, the Merlin, the Peregrine Falcon, and the Gyrfalcon. The Prairie Falcon ranges widely across the western portions of the continent and has been recorded elsewhere as a rare vagrant. Though it is essentially nonmigratory, members of the species do withdraw from the northern limits of the range and from higher elevations at the onset of winter. Some of the population moves farther south into northern Mexico.

Migration

The falcon's direct approach to life carries over into migration. The mountain ridges and their associated updrafts concentrate buteos, eagles, and accipiters during the fall but fail to attract falcons in anything approaching the numbers that appear on the Atlantic Coast. Falcons are capable of sustained long-distance travel using their own powers of flight, soaring on thermals for lift, or combining the two. They have no real need for ridge updrafts and seem disinclined to use them to the extent that other groups of raptors do.

Spring observations from interior ridge sites suggest that most falcons cross ridges rather than following their course. The migration is conducted over a broad front in the interior, and this pattern seems to apply to falcon migration in the fall as well. The birds are widely dispersed and are not easily seen in numbers.

Falcon migration is heaviest along the coasts and is most commonly regarded as an Atlantic Coast phenomenon during the fall. The coastal concentrations of falcons (and of other raptors) have been explained as migratory responses to the barriers presented by large bodies of water. According to the theory, a migrating hawk will circumnavigate a large body of water rather than cross it and will therefore follow the shoreline.

Water barriers do indeed exert a real influence on migration. The Atlantic Ocean causes large numbers of accipiters and buteos to gather at such places as Cape May, New Jersey, and Kiptopeke, Virginia, in the fall and at Sandy Hook, New Jersey, in the spring. The Great Lakes cause birds to congregate at Hawk Ridge, Minnesota, and at Hawk Cliff, Ontario, in the fall and in the spring at Whitefish Point, Michigan, and Derby Hill, New York. Curiously, few falcons are recorded at the sites along the Great Lakes, although accipiters appear there in numbers comparable to those of Atlantic Coast concentrations. Even in the spring, when the Atlantic Coast no longer presents a barrier to northbound birds, many more falcons are recorded at Sandy Hook and on the Texas Gulf Coast than are seen at sites on the southern shores of the Great Lakes.

The barrier theory probably holds little water where falcons are concerned. During fall migration, Merlins and Peregrines are frequently seen well offshore and are commonly observed flying in from the ocean's horizon. Peregrines have been radio tracked as much as 300 miles from land, and Merlins banded in Cape May have been recovered on Bermuda and Cuba.

Kestrels seem more hesitant about traveling any distance over open water, but to what degree this hesitancy is caused by hydrophobia or caution in the face of predation is unknown. Kestrels are frequently attacked by Herring Gulls and Great Black-backed Gulls over open water.

It has been largely overlooked that the Atlantic Coast in the fall and the Gulf Coast in the spring are optimally suited for foraging by a bird with the falcon's style and taste. Both locations have an abundance of avian prey and vast amounts of open space — a natural combination for a bird-eating raptor that hunts unforested flats. Falcons are quite probably not channeled or directed to coastal sites in the same manner as other species of hawks. Instead they selectively concentrate where there is favorable habitat and an abundance of prey.

Our knowledge of another aspect of falcon migration — nocturnal movements — remains largely speculative. Radio-tracked Peregrines have been recorded flying offshore at night, and both Peregrines and Merlins have been seen coming ashore at Cape May at dawn.

Fall migration is protracted. Kestrels, some in heavy molt, begin arriving at coastal locations as early as mid-July. Some birds continue to trickle through during December. The peak of the fall migration occurs between mid-September and mid-October. Most of the migration of Peregrines and Merlins is compressed into the last few days of September and the first 10 days of October.

Identification

Unlike the members of the accipiter tribe, the various falcons have very different plumages. Given good light, close proximity, and enough time, perched birds and flying birds reveal their identities without a struggle. Only occasionally do the old standby field marks fall flat, when the occasional large female Merlin that has an unusually pronounced mustache mark suddenly becomes a Peregrine or when the light-colored, golden-crowned immature *tundrius* Peregrine is transmuted into something exotic by wishful thinking.

But the textbook field points — the double mustache, white bars on the tail, and hood like a football helmet — quickly show their limitations in the hawk-watching arena. Plumage remains an important aid to falcon identification but only on a large scale, in terms of areas of light and dark or in terms of overall color. Even the most distinctly plumaged birds cloak themselves in anonymity when they are far away or when you see them only fleetingly. Each species of falcon offers a number of clues to its identity, and with practice, a hawk watcher can identify even falcons seen at the limit of conjecture.

The Generic Falcon

The falcon is a small-to-medium raptor with long, tapered wings that are pointed at the tip. Color patterns differ, but in general falcons are dark above and barred or streaked below. The throat and chest are usually unmarked or are less heavily marked. The face carries a mustache or sideburn mark that is bold or faint, depending on the species.

Fast, direct flight is the rule. The wing beats are usually continuous, without break or glide. Falcons can and do use thermals for lift and soar very well. When soaring, they look deceptively *un*like falcons.

American Kestrel

The American Kestrel is a Killdeer-sized bird of prey. It is the smallest diurnal raptor in North America and probably the best

Falcons: gliding immatures of all species, backlit.

(A) American Kestrel: long, narrow wings curved back in sickle shape; slight body, narrow tail, small head; overall pale; male shows line of translucent dots on trailing edge of wing.

(B) Merlin: only slightly larger than Kestrel, with broader, straighter, more angular wings; shorter, broader tail; heavier body and larger head; overall dark with white throat and buffy undertail coverts.

(C) Prairie Falcon: long, slim wings, not as angular or as pointed as on Peregrine; body slimmer on average and tail longer than on Peregrine; overall pale brown with translucent flight feathers and white chest, black underwing coverts.

(D) Gyrfalcon: broad, blunt-tipped wings; tail long and broad; head large and body incredibly broad and heavy; plumage extremely variable, from nearly pure white to dark gray; flight feathers translucent and paler than underwing coverts; markings always muted compared with those on other falcons.

(E) Peregrine Falcon: long, angular, sharply pointed wings; rather heavy body; tail relatively shorter than on Merlin; shape and color variable, generally dark with streaked body, pale chest.

Kestrel (*below*) and Merlin approaching.

known. It is familiar to every farm youngster as the hawk that nests "in the hollow oak by the creek" or "under the eaves where the boards are warped." During migration it frequents power-line cuts and perch-hunts from the lines suspended between the towers. In winter, millions of commuters pass Kestrels twice each day as the birds hover-hunt the median strips of interstate highways.

The species is sexually dimorphic (males and females have different plumages, an uncommon trait in raptors). Moreover, the birds are dimorphic from the time they leave the nest. The juvenile plumage worn by other hawks for at least a year sometimes resembles that of the adult female but usually appears unlike the plumage of either adult.

Kestrels consume a varied diet, ranging from crickets to carrion. Insects, small reptiles, and amphibians make up a large part of the prey in summer. After the first frost, they are replaced by small rodents and songbirds up to the size of meadowlarks and the speed of Tree Swallows. Most hunting is done from a perch. Sometimes the bird hover-hunts over a promising piece of cover. Often the two methods are combined. Most prey is taken on the ground by a long, direct approach, but Kestrels will also take birds in flight in true falcon fashion.

At some point in the calendar year, the Kestrel is found in all parts of North America south of the tree line. After the breeding season, it vacates territories in Canada, New England, and northern plains states. On breeding territory, wintering grounds, or in between, it requires open or semiopen country.

IDENTIFICATION. Females are slightly larger than males but not noticeably so. In plumage the male and female are markedly dif-

American Kestrel, underside.
  (A) Male
  (B) Female
Long wings, narrow at base, blunt-tipped in soar; long primaries curve back
in sickle shape during glide. Small and lightweight, with thin body, small
head, long tail. Immatures similar to adults; sexes quite different. Body and
underwing coverts appear pale; male has spots on sides of underparts, a
boldly patterned rufous tail, and a row of translucent dots on trailing edge of
wing. Female has streaked body, fine bars on rufous tail; translucent dots on
wings are faint or absent.

ferent. The rusty backs of the males contrast with their blue
wings. The tails are bright rufous with a broad, dark band near
the tip. Females have reddish brown upperparts, overlaid with
dark, broken barring. Underparts on both sexes are lightly
streaked and spotted, particularly on the sides. Both sexes have
two vertical slashes on the side of the face that resemble a mustache and a sideburn. Immatures are more heavily streaked below
but are similar to adults.

The wings and tail are long and narrow; the body is slight.
Overall the Kestrel appears daintier and more fragile than other
falcons. In normal point-to-point flight, the wings are curved
back in a sickle shape. They are *curved* back, not bent or angled.
Where the wings meet the body, there is often a slight indenta-
tion, an inward pinch along the trailing edge.

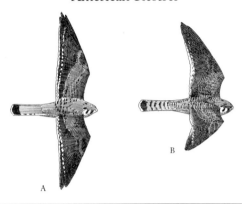

American Kestrel, upperside.
  (A) Male
  (B) Female
Male has rufous back and tail, contrasting with blue-gray wings; female is duller, rusty with dark barring.

In a soar, when the long, tapered wings are fully extended at a right angle to the body, they lack any hard lines or edges. The typically sharp lines of a falcon are softened. The wing tip is blunted like the tip of a pair of safety shears. In overall shape the bird suggests a low-burning candle flame.

Even from a considerable distance, the underparts appear very pale. The mustache and sideburn marks are visible from a distance as well. When the bird is soaring overhead, the fanned tail of the male is bright red, and the single dark band is distinct.

In flight, the male (and sometimes the female) shows a very distinct line of white dots on the trailing edge of the wing (the dots are buff-colored in females), like the luminous rows of lights found on the sides of some deepwater fish.

The flight pattern, very much the product of the bird's shape and size, is light, buoyant, fluttery, somewhat dainty, and wandering. Kestrels glide a great deal more than Merlins and Peregrines. As a result their flight has an accipiterlike quality. Their small size and light weight cause them to be buffeted even by moderate winds.

Merlin flapping: small, angular, and dark. White throat and buffy undertail coverts are often helpful in distinguishing bird from Kestrel at a distance.

Kestrels frequently migrate in small groups of three and four; as many as eight or ten birds may appear in loose flocks along the coast in fall. Kestrel migration is heaviest in the afternoon. Late in the day, Kestrels will sometimes stop migrating for a brief time and will hunt, hovering over an open patch of ground. If they find no prey, they will continue their flight.

Merlin

A Merlin is to a Kestrel what a Harley-Davidson motorcycle is to a scooter. Superficially, the two are similar. Both are small North American falcons that perch-hunt and take a variety of prey. Given the time for study, a Merlin might appear slightly larger but not dramatically so (except for the occasional large female). When a Merlin takes flight, however, all similarities between the two disappear. The difference between them is not just a matter of degree but involves a quantum leap.

A Merlin is a northern breeder that is associated with trees in any numbers only in the nesting season. Even then, it shuns deep forest. It is a bird of the edge and nests in proximity to burns, open meadows, or muskeg. The prairie subspecies (*F. c. richardsonii*) makes use of cottonwoods on the tree-poor plains and appropriates abandoned crow and magpie nests. It has become acclimated to civilization to such an extent that in Saskatoon, Saskatchewan, it nests on residential streets in trees thoughtfully planted by residents and feeds on the abundant House Sparrow (the indicator species of man's strongholds). Outside the breeding season, the Merlin resorts to open spaces in typical falcon fashion: barrier beach, tidal flats, range, and marshland.

Merlins are highly aggressive, pugnacious raptors with little

Merlin chasing Golden Eagle.

tolerance for other birds of prey. They will go out of their way to harass a bird that crosses into their territory or occupies their airspace. Since Merlins seem just as easily provoked during migration as at any other time of year, a Merlin's territory may be inferred to be wherever it happens to find itself.

Surprisingly, in at least one location, wintering Merlins are known to roost in a communal fashion. Each evening, between eight and ten birds gather along the road that leads to the end of a sandy spit before retiring into a small holly forest at dusk. At dawn, the birds disperse to hunt and feed.

IDENTIFICATION. Male Merlins are only slightly larger than Kestrels. Females can be larger than pigeons. First-year birds and females are dark brown above, with heavy streaking on the underparts, which contrasts with a white throat. The net effect at a distance is of a small dark falcon.

Adult males are a bright, metallic blue above, lighter and more finely streaked below. At a distance, males appear very pale — as pale as a Kestrel. In all plumages, the mustache mark is faint, smudgy, and indistinct. At close range, dark tails show many pencil-thin white bands.

The Merlin is stocky, angular, and powerful, the Porsche Carrera of the falcon clan. The body is chestier and heavier than that of a Kestrel. The tail appears shorter. The wings are longer and broader. In a full soar, they are shaped like isosceles triangles and meet the body flush and broad. The wing tip is sharply pointed. The lines of the bird are hard and angular.

Immatures and adult females look dark overall at any dis-

Merlin, underside.
  (A) Adult male
  (B) Immature
  (C) Immature
Small, dark, and angular, with relatively short, very pointed wings, fairly long tail, large head. In soar (A) wings are held as clean triangles. In all flight attitudes there is a slight step from the outermost secondary to the slightly shorter innermost primary. Plumage variation is not pronounced; all birds are dark, with checkered underwing, streaked body, black tail with fine white bands, and contrasting white throat and buffy undertail coverts. Variations include lightly streaked adult male (A) with pale face and dark, heavily streaked, hooded immatures (B, C), with adult females in between.

tance — chocolate falcons. The white throat and pale, buffy undertail coverts contrast with the rest of the bird.

Seen from below, in a soar, the bird shows wings that are boldly checkered in black and white. The folded tail exhibits fine, white bands at close range, but on high-flying birds the tail will be uniformly pale from the wings to midpoint and uniformly dark from the midpoint to the tip.

The flight of a Merlin is its most distinctive feature. Point-to-point flight is pure and direct. The wing beats are quick, continuous, and powerful, short, pistonlike strokes. All of the power

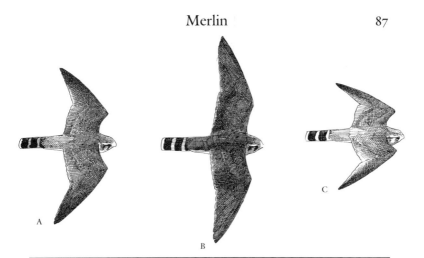

Merlin, upperside.
(A) Adult male (*F. c. columbarius*)
(B) Immature
(C) Adult male (*F. c. richardsoni*)

Adult males blue above with pale rump, extremely pale powder blue in prairie race *richardsoni*. Females have similar pattern in gray-brown; immatures are uniformly dark chocolate brown.

seems concentrated in the flicking downstroke. The cadence and motion are not unlike those of a domestic pigeon.

The flight does not wander, but Merlins will sometimes accelerate and drop low to cruise-hunt over a likely looking piece of cover. In flight they often barely clear the top of the vegetation. Along hawk-watch sites on the interior ridges, Merlins are rarely seen approaching. They appear and disappear before anyone can say "Merlin." They come from below, and the silhouette of a small dark falcon is lost against the backdrop of trees.

Merlins are usually solitary (because they have a bad disposition) and will frequently go out of their way to harass other birds in migration. A Merlin's aggressive behavior may be used as a field identification point and as a means of detection. At Cape May, high-flying Merlins are usually detected because they are harassing another raptor.

MERLIN SUBSPECIES. The Richardson's or Prairie Merlin (*F. c. richardsoni*) is larger, paler, and more finely marked than the nominate race. It is a prairie specialty, breeding in Alberta, Saskatchewan, Montana, and North Dakota and wintering extensively in Oklahoma and the Texas panhandle.

The female is pale gray-brown above and streaked with tan below — very unlike the darker eastern Merlin but not so dissimilar as to lack the characteristic Merlin field marks. Large females appear almost as big as male Prairie Falcons (though no overlap occurs). Size, coupled with the common traits of pale plumage and the habit of blasting low across prairies, makes it easy to confuse the female Richardson's Merlin with Prairie Falcons.

Male Richardson's are pale powder blue above and tan with reddish streaks below, an eastern Merlin overexposed by two f-stops. Immatures are uniformly chocolate brown.

The Black Merlin (*F. c. suckleyii*) is found in the forested coastal regions of British Columbia and Vancouver Island. It winters to central California.

Although the Black Merlin is slightly larger than the nominate race, and considerably darker, it is not always readily distinguished from *F. c. columbarius*. Females are virtually black above and dark brown and heavily streaked below. Males are charcoal gray above and on the average are darker below than the birds of the nominate race.

Peregrine Falcon

The Peregrine Falcon, a medium-sized raptor, has long been a source of inspiration. At one time, during the Middle Ages, it denoted social status; only lords could fly a Peregrine from the fist. More recently, the bird has served as a rallying point and as evidence of the impact of pesticides on the environment. Other considerations aside, the Peregrine Falcon is a creature whose awesome mastery of its element sets new standards for the word "perfection." Few works of nature or man equal the sight of a Peregrine in the wind.

All three North American races are cliff-nesting raptors. The arboreal race, *F. p. anatum,* once commonly nested east of the

Adult Peregrine flapping.

Mississippi and lived well on the Passenger Pigeon, its principal prey item. No one knows how many Peregrines occupied how many ledges 150 years ago, but it seems safe to assume that, after the demise of its once-abundant source of food, the Peregrine population declined. An inventory published in 1941 found a total of 212 nest ledges occupied east of the Mississippi. By 1970, the Peregrine had been functionally (if not totally) exterminated by DDT in its eastern strongholds, and its numbers had been seriously reduced in the Rockies. The arctic populations were reduced by half.

At present, the breeding range of Peregrine Falcons in North America is limited to arctic regions of Greenland, Canada, and Alaska (*F. p. tundrius*), the Pribilof Islands off the coast of Alaska (*F. p. pealei*), and several river systems in Alaska, the Yukon, and the Northwest Territories (*F. p. anatum*). These populations are healthy and increasing. The bird also nests in the Rockies and along the West Coast. For better or worse, restocking attempts have been made in the East. The Peregrine has gained a foothold in coastal marshes in New Jersey and beneath major bridge structures.

Peregrines winter along the Atlantic Coast, from New York through South America. On the Pacific Coast, Peregrines winter from the Alaskan panhandle to points south. Tundra birds, the most migratory, winter in Central and South America.

The Peregrine's diet is almost exclusively avian. Its preferred modes of hunting include the long tail-chase over open country and the long power-stoop. The target of such a specialized mode of hunting most often wears feathers, but Peregrines are not

Peregrine Falcon, underside.
  (A) Adult
  (B) Immature
Medium to large bird; long-winged and fairly long-tailed. In soar, wings are
held straight with evenly curved edges, tail fanned broadly; wings may appear
blunt-tipped in soar but at all other times are sharply pointed. Variable.
Males can be small, slim, and buoyant; the largest females are broad, heavy,
and powerful. Adults are light-chested, with fine barring on belly, heavy black
mustache; immatures are streaked on body (some heavily, some lightly) and
have distinct brown mustache, sometimes very thin in pale *tundrius* birds. In
all plumages the wings and tail are dark and clean-edged.

averse to taking bats during daylight hours. Nor are they above
pirating a Harrier's mouse if the opportunity presents itself.
    The reduced use of DDT in North America, together with the
proliferation of the species's most resistant individuals, has recently brought a dramatic and rapid recovery in the Peregrine
populations occupying tundra and northern river areas. In Eng-

A

B

Peregrine Falcon, upperside.
  (A) Immature (*F. p. tundrius*)
  (B) Adult
Adult slaty slue, palest on rump (males paler and bluer), with dark wing tips, tail tip, and head markings, but uniformly dark. Immature is uniformly dark brown except for some fine light edges on scapulars and pale buffy crown on *tundrius,* as illustrated.

land, where populations were severely reduced as well, the recovery of the bird is now complete. Concern for the North American Peregrine continues and will do so as long as DDT is applied in the tropics where the bird winters. Given time and the absence of human folly, the bird may again populate the nest ledges of its historic range.

IDENTIFICATION. The Peregrine is a medium-to-large falcon with a wide range in size between the small male and the larger female. Adults and immatures differ in plumage. Young birds have brown backs, heavily streaked underparts, and a buff-colored chest and throat. Adults are uniformly blue-gray above and heavily barred below, with a gleaming white chest and throat. Immature birds of the tundra subspecies, the one most likely to be seen in migration in the East, also have a blond crown and nape. Both adults and immatures have a bold, distinct mustache mark.

The Peregrine is an extremely long-winged and fairly long-tailed falcon. Immatures have longer tails than adults. The body is heavy and broad, and the wings seem narrow. The tail, when closed, is still very broad.

A soaring bird has wings that are tapered both fore and aft, so that they resemble long, tapered candles or an elongated lancet arch. The outer tail feathers, when fully fanned, form a semicircle and nearly touch the trailing edge of the wing.

The wing beat is fluid, rhythmic, elastic, and whiplike. The flap, which looks very shallow, seems to roll down the long wing in undulating pulses. In cadence and execution the wing beat is not unlike that of a Common Loon.

Though they are usually solitary, Peregrines often migrate in pairs.

Curiously, the bird most often confused with the Peregrine is not even a falcon. The Northern Harrier is, in fact, similar in size, but its long wings lack the Peregrine's broadness and taper. The Harrier's tail is also much longer than that of a Peregrine.

A soaring Peregrine also bears an uncanny likeness to a soaring Broad-winged Hawk. The broad tail of the Peregrine offsets or masks the wing length, producing a silhouette very much like that of a Broad-winged Hawk (and very unlike the picture of a falcon).

PEREGRINE SUBSPECIES. In North America, three different subspecies of Peregrine Falcon are recognized. The *F. p. anatum* now nests only in the western half of the United States (west of the plains) and north through Canada and Alaska to the tree line. The eastern breeding population has disappeared, though the bird probably occurs as a fall migrant along the East Coast.

The adult *anatum* Peregrine is dark gray to black above and heavily barred below except for a pure white upper chest and throat. The lower chest and belly commonly bear a rufous wash, so that the bird has a subtle orange or pinkish cast when seen from below. The dark upperparts extend helmetlike onto the head and face. The black mustache stripe is sharply defined, bold, and obvious. Immatures are generally dark chocolate below; some boast a faint rusty wash.

The tundra Peregrine (*F. p. tundrius*) is a comparatively pale bird. This arctic subspecies, wintering in the tropics, is the bird most commonly seen in migration and is distinctly paler than most *anatum* birds. Adults are light gray above. Some individuals show a blue-gray cast on the back and tail. The paler tones, coupled with a more restricted facial pattern, mute the bold helmeted or capped appearance of the *anatum*. The barring on the underparts is faint and fine — almost a vermiculation. On some birds, particularly adult males, the barring may be so fine that even individuals seen at moderate heights appear to have pure white underparts. The rusty wash is absent.

Plumage on immature tundra birds is highly variable. Underparts range from chocolate to tan. Some individuals are almost as pale above and below as a Prairie Falcon. Almost all immature tundra birds have a distinct blond crown.

Whether they are adults or immatures, tundra birds appear to have longer wings and tails than *anatum* Peregrines. Tundra birds look rangier. Though the birds have similar measurements, the *anatum* Peregrine *appears* stockier (perhaps because of the relative width of the wings or the tail).

The third North American Peregrine, the Peale's race (*F. p. pealeii*), is a bird of Pacific Northwest coastal reaches. It is not nomadically inclined and usually winters no farther south than central California. This subspecies shares with the Gyrfalcon both size and plumage traits; the two are easily confused.

The adult Peale's is dark gray to black above and heavily barred below. The rusty wash of *anatum* is absent. The cap is full. Adults are easily recognized as Peregrines; the immature plumage is the source of difficulty. Upperparts range from dark brown to black in some birds; streaking on the underparts is often so heavy that it fuses into a solid, dark mass. The mustache stripe, the hallmark of a Peregrine, spreads to form a solid, dark face. The bird is a Gyrfalcon look-alike.

Restricted range and sedentary nature reduce the identification problem. Be aware, however, that artificial introduction programs have established pure Peale's and Peale's hybrids (not to mention a few exotic Peregrine subspecies) in the East. As a result it is exceptionally difficult to identify the subspecies of Peregrines breeding in the East.

If you see a large dark falcon, wing shape, body bulk, tail length and shape, manner of flight, and the time of year will help you differentiate the Gyrfalcon from immature Peale's Peregrines.

Prairie Falcon

If you have the good fortune to be a westerner, then you are no doubt familiar with a butte-haunting ghost of a falcon, the prairie wraith. The bird is a spirit in league with shortgrass prairie, towering buttes, sandstone cliffs, open sage, alkali flats, and alpine tundra. In such a habitat, your chances of seeing the bird are high. Beyond a range that extends roughly from the shortgrass plains westward to the coast, north to southern Manitoba, Alberta, and British Columbia, and south (during colder months) into Mexico, your chances of seeing the bird are little better than your chances of spotting a real ghost.

The Prairie Falcon is most often likened to a pale Peregrine, an understandable but not terribly just analogy. It is easier to become familiar with something by measuring it against a known quantity, and the Peregrine's greater range and mobility make it the more familiar bird over most of North America.

But the Prairie Falcon is a bird in a class by itself. It is more active than a Peregrine, more nervous, and more aggressive to-

Typical view of Prairie Falcon.

ward other raptors. It always seems to be going somewhere else and to have been glimpsed just a bit too late.

Prairie Falcons have refined two favorite hunting styles, both suited to terrain where everything that moves above the horizon is noted by all things that are living and want to stay that way. One technique employs the calculated use of terrain; the other, the element of surprise.

From a windmill, from a nest ledge, or from the air, the bird makes its prey, takes wing, and flies rapidly along a route calculated to conceal its approach for as long as possible. The flight is usually low and hugs the ground.

The same low, swift, coursing flight is also used to locate prey. A Prairie Falcon on patrol will cruise low over suitable terrain to avoid detection, hoping to surprise a ground squirrel or to flush a Horned Lark. Less frequently (though with no less skill), the Prairie Falcon will hunt from a soar, in the manner of a Peregrine, executing a long, calculated, shallow stoop on sighted prey.

Not surprisingly, in view of the bird's style of hunting, Prairie Falcons are usually sighted when they are traveling from one place to another at grass-top levels. Also understandably, most sightings are brief in duration; the bird is either coming (if you are lucky) or going (if you are not).

Prairie Falcons depart from the well-developed migratory tendencies of the other four falcons in this book. They are birds of the western plains, and they stay there. Birds abandon the higher elevations, and some vacate the northern portions of the species's range. But the Prairie Falcon is not a migrant as Merlins or Peregrines are. Beginning in late August, Prairie Falcons relocate to areas that offer the promise of a stable source of prey, some wandering south into Mexico.

IDENTIFICATION. The Prairie Falcon is the size of a Peregrine and is very similar in shape and proportions. In the hawk-watching arena, adult and immature plumages are functionally identical. Adults are gray-brown above and paler than a Peregrine; immatures lack the gray overtones. Sexes differ only in size.

The term "sandy" has often been misapplied to the bird's plum-

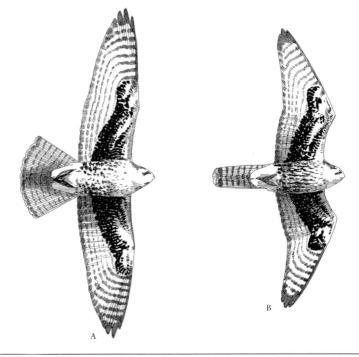

Prairie Falcon, underside.
  (A) Adult
  (B) Immature
Average bird is slimmer and longer-tailed than Peregrine, but the two probably overlap. Wing tips slightly more rounded. Best identified by plumage, much paler than on Peregrine; all flight feathers translucent with light gray markings. Body mostly white (adults) or buffy (immatures), although the most heavily marked individuals can show a complete blackish belly band; face markings narrow and brown. Most of the underwing coverts are spotted and barred black; the resulting black bar along the underwing is conspicuous and diagnostic. There is little plumage variation, but immatures are buffier, with more streaking below.

age. "Sandy" has a wide range of interpretations, from beach white to river-bottom brown, but it usually denotes the lighter end of the scale — a color too light to describe a Prairie Falcon accurately. Most Prairie Falcons are darker except for the tail, which is pale and contrasts noticeably with the darker upperparts. A Peregrine shows no such contrast.

Prairie Falcon, upperside.
Adult and immature are similar: always brown, darkest on primaries, paler on rump and tail (outer tail feathers palest). Immature Peregrine is brown above but much darker and more uniform, with a slaty cast.

The underparts of adults are cream-colored and lightly spotted; those of immatures are buffy and streaked (most heavily along the side of the chest, the flanks, the belly, and particularly the legs in most individuals). The mustache stripe is a thin version of a Peregrine's broad sideburn slash.

The most conspicuous plumage characteristic is the bold, dark to black triangles that form an inner core on the bird's pale wings. The dark area is *not* limited to the axillars (the wing pits) but runs prominently down the trailing edge of the underwing coverts, as if the bird had two broad, black support struts. These wing linings are visible at tremendous distances, seem particularly distinct in poor light, and, in the case of high-soaring, backlit birds, may be the only visible distinguishing marks as the pale outline of the bird disappears against a bright sky. The triangles are not found on any other North American falcon; they are definitive, a distinctive field mark on both adults and immatures.

The Prairie Falcon is not as heavily built as a Peregrine, and its body is more tube-shaped. The tail is long, surprisingly broad, and uncommonly blunt. The wings are as long as those of a Peregrine but differ in proportions. The "arm" is long; the "hand" appears short. Though the Prairie Falcon's wing is not necessarily narrower than that of a Peregrine, it appears relatively emaciated and flaccid. It lacks the clean, tempered lines of the Peregrine wing.

Prairie Falcons prefer gliding to soaring and as a result are commonly seen with the hands pulled slightly back. But even in a full soar, the wing tip is not as pointed as it would be on a Peregrine. In part, the reason is the middle primaries, which bulge outward near the end of the wing, blunting the tip and imparting a sense of softness and rounded curves.

When the slim body, long tail, thin and softly curved, back-swept wings, and pale underparts are all taken together, the bird looks very much like a large, soaring American Kestrel (and may easily be mistaken for one).

In flight, the rhythm and cadence of the Prairie Falcon are like those of a Peregrine, but the movement and its mechanics are different. The Peregrine's wing beat is a fluid, undulating ripple of movement down the length of the wing. The wing beat of a Prairie Falcon is stiff and mechanical. The motion seems centered at midwing, at the wrist. The wrist moves in short, stiff, up-and-down strokes. The wing beat of a Prairie Falcon combines the cadence of a Peregrine's flap with the mechanical qualities of a Short-eared Owl's flight.

Gyrfalcon

The Gyrfalcon is a bird of fire and ice, a bird that combines the size of a Red-tailed Hawk with the flight prowess of a Merlin and adds an element beyond the measure of both. This is a true arctic falcon. Males occasionally winter on their nest ledges as far north as the Brooks Range in Alaska, although most adults vacate the high arctic breeding areas and move south to the tree line. Immatures wander farther south on occasion, but even in southern Canada and northern border states, the bird is rare.

The size of the bird and its broad proportions, unlike those of a falcon, make it appear deceptively slow. It is not. A Peregrine, for all its speed, must capture its prey in a long tail chase or relies on a meteoric stoop that capitalizes on surprise. The Gyr simply flies prey down. Only the Gyrfalcon is capable of overtaking waterfowl as fast as Pintails or Wigeons in full flight. Its design makes this bird the equal of anything on wings.

Gyrfalcon (*left*) soaring with Red-tailed Hawk.

IDENTIFICATION. The Gyrfalcon is a large, robust falcon as big as or bigger than a large female Peregrine. There is sexual dimorphism in Peregrines and Gyrfalcons, however, and male Gyrfalcons are commonly smaller than Peale's Peregrines (*F. p. pealei*), the dark subspecies found in coastal Alaska. Female Gyrfalcons are massive, easily larger than the largest Red-tailed Hawk.

Three general color phases are recognized: white, gray, and dark. These phases are plumage tendencies more than absolute forms. Variations between color phases commonly occur.

White-phase adults are white overall, with some dark flecking on the upperparts and little, if any, patterning below. Wing tips are dark both above and below. Gray-phase adults have gray backs, with lighter edges on the feathers that create a scaled effect on wings and back. Underparts are white with dark flecking on the underwing coverts and belly. Head and chest contrast with the darker back and underparts. The single mustache mark is indistinct but becomes more pronounced near the chin. Dark-phase

Gyrfalcon, underside.
   (A) Gray phase
   (B) White phase
Large, broad, heavy-bodied; wings unfalconlike when soaring, broad and
distinctly rounded; tail long and broad; head large. White phase unmistakable
(but beware of albinos of other species, particularly Red-taileds, which are
more likely than white Gyrfalcons to occur in, say, Alabama); white plumage
relieved only by black tips on primaries and fine black barring on flanks. Dark
phases distinguished from Peregrine and Goshawk by dark underwing
coverts, contrasting with pale gray flight feathers; by generally muted, pale
pattern without sharply defined dark markings; and by shape (see next
figure).

birds are smoky brown above and heavily spotted below (almost
dark). Flight feathers are light and appear translucent from below.
Mustache marks are often lost against the dark patterns on the
face but sometimes become distinct near the chin.

Gyrfalcon, upperside.
  (A) White phase
  (B) Gray phase
In characteristic flight posture this falcon exhibits hunched shoulders, drooping head and tail, broad back, crooked wings. White birds are more heavily marked above than below. Bird shown in (A) is near the light extreme, with only faint barring on back and wing coverts; others are evenly barred from crown to rump and appear gray; all have black wing tips. Dark birds may look spotted or uniform, all in various shades of smoky gray or brown.

Immature birds are darker and more patterned than adults. Immatures are also most commonly sighted in areas south of their normal wintering range.

This is a large, heavy, hunch-backed, barrel-bodied falcon. The wings are long and broad, particularly along the arm. The wing is less tapered than the wing of a Peregrine, and the wing tips are more blunt. The tail is long, very broad, and very heavy. From below, the tail's length is masked by its extreme width, but when viewed wing-on, the tail's length is strikingly apparent.

Though in shape and proportions a Gyrfalcon is unusual

among falcons, its flight is very falconlike — direct and incredibly swift. The wing beats are rapid and constant. The motion of the wing appears limited to the hands alone. The wings look motionless; all movement is concentrated in the rapid flicking of the wing tips. The flight suggests a Merlin more than a Peregrine.

Because of its size and overall shape, the Gyr is most commonly confused with the Peregrine, but note the differences in proportions! Another bird that bears surprising resemblance to the Gyrfalcon is the Goshawk, which is also large, with long, broad wings and tail. The wings, when partly closed, appear very falconlike. A simple rule of thumb will usually separate Gyrfalcons from Goshawks quickly: if it goes into the trees, it isn't a Gyrfalcon.

Telling Falcons Apart

Falcon identification, unlike that of accipiters, is not a hair-splitting feat. Each falcon has distinct differences in plumage, shape, and flight. But these birds may be more complicated to identify than accipiters. With accipiters, you need to distinguish a Sharp-shinned from Cooper's or Cooper's from a Goshawk. Kestrels, Merlins, Peregrines, and Prairie Falcons share so many traits that any one may be confused with any of the other three. The Gyrfalcon is seldom seen in most locations but may certainly be confused with immature Peregrines and Prairie Falcons.

An approaching falcon has a distinctive wing beat and manner of flight. The wing beats will usually be steady and uninterrupted. Buteos, accipiters, and Harriers flap in a series and then glide, or if they are using a strong updraft off a ridge, they will have their wings tucked in and will not be flapping at all.

Falcons beat steadily as a rule although Kestrels tend not to do so on calm days or in light winds. Each species has its own distinctive cadence or manner of flight. Even when distance makes size, color, and shape impossible to determine, the cadence and rhythm of a falcon's flight will identify it.

An approaching Peregrine will look very long in the wing. The movement of the wings is shallow, fluid, rhythmic, and undulating. The wing beat appears leisurely, but the bird covers ground amazingly fast. If the bird glides at all, the glide will often be held for a long time.

The wing beat of a Prairie Falcon is stiffer than that of a Peregrine. It has the same cadence but lacks the fluid quality. The difference is like that between a sprinter and a speed skater. A Prairie Falcon's wing moves at the wrist, flexing up and down in a mechanical fashion. Prairie Falcons are ground huggers; Peregrines prefer the heights.

If you are fortunate enough to see an approaching Merlin (Merlins usually appear without much warning), you will see a small, dark, short-winged object moving at astounding speed. The wing beats will be quick, constant, downward-flicking pistonlike strokes. The flight will be direct and steady, but the bird will often dodge left or right or will drop a few feet to hug the contour of a hedgerow, a tree line, or the crest of a ridge. Merlins will also jump quickly to the left or right to snatch an insect in flight and will go well out of their way to harass other birds of prey. *Rule of thumb: if a bird passes a perched raptor and doesn't take a shot at it, then it isn't a Merlin.*

A distant Kestrel will appear small, slim, and long-winged. The wing beats will be fluttery, with lots of up-and-down motion at the tip. They might be intermittent and punctuated with a short glide (as in a Sharp-skinned Hawk), particularly on windless days. A Kestrel's flight is buoyant and wandering; the bird often fails to keep an even keel. But in a strong headwind, a Kestrel will pull its wings in and pump strongly. In this attitude, a Kestrel is very like a Merlin.

The overhead silhouette of a highballing Peregrine can be confusing. An adult male with its wings pulled in, beating steadily, may disconcertingly resemble a large female Merlin. The flowing motion of a Peregrine's wing movement is not evident from below, but the wings and tail of a Peregrine will be noticeably broader than those of a Merlin. A Peregrine's tail will taper toward the tip; a Merlin's tail usually does not taper and is always narrower. A Prairie Falcon's tail has the length of a Merlin, the untapered breadth of a Peregrine, and a squared bluntness that recalls a Gyrfalcon.

Look for color. From below, a Prairie Falcon will be a pale, tawny outline surrounding two prominent black wing struts. A female or immature Merlin will appear all dark, with perhaps a hint of whiteness on the throat. A Peregrine, particularly an adult, will look very white-chested — a helpful feature, since the adults have shorter wings and are therefore more Merlin-like in overall shape.

Going by, wing-on, a Merlin loses none of its bullet Gestalt. Even at a distance, it seems dark overall. A Kestrel appears lighter, particularly on the underparts, and a hint of rufous is often visible. *Caution: although Merlins are dark and Kestrels are light, this rule does not apply to adult male Merlins. Adult male Merlins appear pale at a distance, but in most locations they represent only a fraction of the birds seen on migration, and they migrate later than most of the falcons in the fall (adult male Merlins migrate in mid to late October along the Atlantic Coast). Adult male Merlins are particularly squat, stubby, and speedy; Kestrels are slimmer and longer-limbed. These differences should help you distinguish between the two birds at a distance.*

Though a Kestrel may appear Merlin-like as it pumps into a headwind, because of its inferior weight it just can't buck the wind as well. It will move more slowly than its larger, heavier relative.

From below, the Merlin still appears dark, and the bold checkerboard pattern of the underwings is visible. Male Kestrels will display a white row of dots on the trailing edge of the wing. Female Kestrels and Merlins may bear indistinct, tawny-colored dots, but distinct, white dots automatically denote a male Kestrel.

Distinguishing Merlins from Kestrels when the birds are high overhead is probably the toughest identification problem facing hawk watchers. Hard angles (Merlins) are no longer distinct from soft angles (Kestrels). Behavior probably offers the best clue. Most high-flying Merlins are detected because an observant hawk watcher sees a small falcon suddenly accelerate and pursue another raptor. Plumage is virtually useless as a clue. The overall impression of darkness still holds for a Merlin, but it is not obvious and is usually noted *after* careful study. The tail patterns on the two birds are different and worth noting. The closed tail of a

Merlin is evenly divided between dark and light. From the wings to the midpoint, the tail is pale; from the midpoint to the tip, it is dark. The tail on a distant Kestrel shows no such demarcation.

In a soar, a Kestrel will have long, narrow, softly curved wings that resemble a long, round-tipped candle flame; the tail appears long and narrow. A Merlin will have wings that look like broad, sharply cut isosceles triangles; the tail is short and not as thin. A Peregrine will have wings that look like long, graceful, tapered candlesticks. The closed tail will appear long, broad, and tapered toward the tip. Prairie Falcons usually pull their wing tips back, but even when the wings are fully extended, the tips are rounded, like those of a Kestrel, and the tail is broad and blunt.

Kites

Graceful Masters of the Southern Summer Skies

S P E C I E S

Mississippi Kite, *Ictinia mississippiensis*
American Swallow-tailed Kite, *Elanoides forficatus*
Black-shouldered Kite, *Elanus caeruleus*

In Europe, Asia, and Africa, "kite" brings to mind a carrion-eating bird, but in the Western Hemisphere it largely denotes a small, insect-eating raptor. The term probably comes from the Aryan root *skut,* meaning "to go swiftly" (an apt description of the way most kites swoop on their prey), although in current use the word describes a way of hanging motionless in the air. A Red-tailed Hawk, for example, can *kite* in the wind. North American kites as a group contain such diverse species as the Snail Kite and the Hook-billed Kite, neither of which is migratory. The three North American kites of open areas (the Mississippi, Swallow-tailed, and Black-shouldered kites) display remarkable energy and spirit and are highly social (even during the breeding season). Their gregariousness is particularly apparent during migration, when 500 to 600 Mississippi Kites have been seen together and as many as 150 Swallow-taileds have gathered in a single flock in southern Florida.

Kites are agile, at times vigorous, and always graceful. They are known for their protracted soaring and hunting on the wing for as many as 10 hours a day. They soar to great heights and can be seen as tiny dots against the billowing summer cumulus. All are birds of southern distribution. The Mississippi Kite and Swallow-tailed Kite are highly migratory and withdraw to Central and South America during the North American winter. All species prefer open spaces: the Swallow-tailed is the graceful aerialist of the Everglades, the Mississippi is as much at home on the Santee River delta in South Carolina as on the Kansas prairies, and the Black-shouldered Kite hunts over the Rio Grande in Texas or the arid rangeland of Los Padres National Forest, California.

Migration

Even though kites move great distances outside their normal range (either as dispersing young in the summer and early fall or as overshoots and prospecting adults in the spring), kite migration in the real sense is confined to the southern states in which the birds breed. Great flocks of Mississippi Kites are seen along the east coast of Mexico and Texas in both spring and fall; vast flocks have been seen in Panama as well. They are highly social. A group is as likely to be seen as one bird, both within the bird's normal range and occasionally outside it. Individuals wander widely in the spring; 8–10 kites occur at Cape May in May and June, and the bird is almost annual on Cape Cod. In the East the Mississippi Kite is decidedly coastal, and there are few interior records. The birds can be characterized as late spring and early fall migrants, and the migratory flocks may be quite high in the air.

Swallow-taileds are less conspicuous when migrating, and in fact their population is much smaller. Nevertheless, great flocks of as many as 150 birds are seen in southern Florida annually in February and March and in August before they move on to Cuba. A few take the Texas and Gulf Coast route, and numbers of birds are seen in Panama, where some are migrants and many are local. Swallow-tailed Kites are decidedly coastal as well; many are often seen over barrier islands. They cross water without hesitation.

Both the Swallow-tailed and the Black-shouldered kites are known wanderers. Each year single birds appear far beyond their normal ranges. Nonetheless, they are virtually never seen at established autumn hawk watches because they leave in early fall before observations begin.

The Black-shouldered Kite is largely nonmigratory, but its range is expanding, and its propensity for wandering is plain. The bird is now breeding in Florida and commonly appears in areas of the Southwest, outside its nesting range. It has been included in this book because it tends to roam.

Identification

In most of this book, "identification" means distinguishing one species from others in the same grouping that are closely related. Identifying a Red-tailed Hawk, for example, is largely a matter of distinguishing it from other species of buteos. Identifying a Cooper's Hawk means distinguishing it from a Sharp-shinned Hawk or a Goshawk. Kites are a different matter.

The three species covered here are easily separated, the Swallow-tailed Kite by size and shape, the Mississippi Kite and the Black-shouldered Kite by plumage, behavior, and, over most of North America, distribution and seasonality. To identify kites successfully you need to be able to distinguish distant kites from *other* birds (including some that are not even raptors).

The Generic Kite

A kite is a slim, finely proportioned, medium-sized raptor with long, falconlike wings and a long tail that twists and turns in flight. Its colors are shades of white and black and gray.

The flight is light, buoyant, acrobatic, and incomparably graceful. The wing beat is slow, stiff, and deliberate. Flight is the bird's natural state. With its distinctive plumage and shape, coupled with its unique manner of flight, the kite usually poses no identification puzzle. But there is one exception to this rule.

Mississippi Kite

It was September 19, 1980, at Cape May Point, the very beginning of falcon season, the time when Peregrines may be expected on a daily basis. The conditions were perfect: wind north, bordering on northeast, and numerous hazy clouds overhead — a good wind for Peregrines and a fine day for spotting distant birds. First one, then a second, and a third Peregrine came on.

The distant, falcon-shaped bird, backlit to the east, was sailing, gliding, and quartering the wind toward the crowd of hawk watchers at the Point. As it approached, it more and more as-

Kites: gliding immatures of all species.

(A) American Swallow-tailed Kite
(B) Black-shouldered Kite
(C) Mississippi Kite

These species are difficult to confuse with each other; Swallow-tailed and Black-shouldered are difficult to confuse with any other bird. Mississippi Kite is easily confused with male Peregrine Falcon, but notice slightly flared tail with narrow pale bands, short outermost primary, different head pattern, unbarred primaries and secondaries, wings narrower at base than at wrist, and different flight style.

sumed the characteristics of a classic Peregrine — long tapered wings, long tail, and the pale head and chocolate brown color that identified it as an immature tundra Peregrine. As small and slender as it was, the bird had to be a tiercel.

Finally, at point-blank range, the bird took three stiff, deep flaps, kited (stalled), caught a dragonfly, and began soaring leisurely over the open-mouthed crowd. It calmly consumed its prey on the wing — uncommon behavior for a Peregrine but just av-

Mississippi Kite going away.

erage for a Mississippi Kite. This was the second autumn record of a Mississippi Kite in the history of Cape May hawk watching.

The Mississippi Kite has a wide range across the southern United States. It can be quite conspicuous in the shelter-belt habitats of Texas and Oklahoma but remarkably secretive in the southern swamps of Georgia and South Carolina. It is a deceptively small raptor at rest, appearing no larger than an American Kestrel. In flight, though, the long wings give it a wingspan roughly as great as that of the Broad-winged Hawk. During migration, Mississippi Kites form large flocks that pass through southern Texas primarily during late August and early September and return relatively late in April and May.

These kites eat insects. Virtually all of their food is caught in the air as they dive and perform spectacular aerial maneuvers. After soaring gracefully and gaining altitude, a kite will execute a spectacular dive on a dragonfly, pull out at treetop level, and then placidiy eat while circling on the wing.

IDENTIFICATION. The Mississippi Kite, a medium-sized, falcon-like bird, has the size, proportions, and shape of a Peregrine. Adults, in bright sun, are light gray and distinctly white-headed. The tail is uniformly dark, above and below. The pale secondaries form a bright white patch on the trailing edge of the upper surface of the wing — a mark that is far more obvious than most field guides indicate.

Immatures are somewhat variable in plumage, ranging from

Adult Mississippi Kite catching dragonfly.

sandy tan (with darker streaking) to dark chocolate brown all over (with little streaking). Subadults may be all dark gray or brownish gray throughout, with no streaking at all. Both immature and subadult birds have distinctive black and white barring on the tails, perfect slotted windows.

The body is long, narrow, slight. The wings are long (extending beyond the tip of the tail when the bird is perched), slim, and tapered *but* oddly proportioned. The arms are narrow, the hands, broad (like overdeveloped forearms). The leading edge bulges forward at the wrist, and the trailing edge is straight cut when the bird is gliding (which it usually is). In shape the wing is similar to that of a Broad-winged Hawk in a glide posture. The outermost primary is extremely short — a fine point but a very visible one.

The tail is long and splays outward toward the square-cut tip. The flaring of the outer tail feathers is evident whether the tail is closed or partially fanned.

Mississippi Kite, underside.

(A) Immature

(B) Adult

Slim, long-winged, medium-sized, with slender body and fairly long tail. Wings are narrow-armed and broad-handed, with distinctly short outermost primary. Tail flares slightly at tip and is constantly spread and twisted in flight. Adult is gray-bodied with darker underwings, black tail, and whitish head. Immature has body and underwing coverts buffy, with dark streaking and spotting of variable density; may be lighter or darker than illustrated; tail has several narrow light bands; flight feathers dark gray, with pale bases on outermost primaries; dark cheek patch sets off pale eyestripe. Distinguished from immature Peregrine by shape and flight style, narrow pale bands in tail, head pattern, and pale bases on outermost primaries.

Mississippi Kite, upperside.
(A) Immature
(B) Adult
Bright silvery secondaries of adult diminish with wear and are inconspicuous by late summer; wing coverts and all feathers of back are edged with buffy on immature, unlike plain gray-brown back of Peregrine.

The wing beat of a Mississippi Kite is stiff and deliberate, with little movement or flexibility down the length of the wing. The bird gives the impression of flapping only as a last resort — when the alternative to staying aloft is falling out of the sky. It commonly flaps only in tight maneuvers or when it wants to accelerate quickly to capture prey.

In addition, the Mississippi Kite is not fond of soaring. Sailing and gliding are the preferred mode of locomotion.

American Swallow-tailed Kite

Few would dispute that the Swallow-tailed Kite is the most graceful flier of any raptor in North America. It will glide and float

Kites

American Swallow-tailed Kite.

over rice fields endlessly, turn and ride the light breeze to catch dragonflies eaten on the wing, and only rarely flap or soar.

Swallow-taileds quarter the wind flawlessly, in total aerial control. In comparison with Mississippi Kites, they fly in slow motion; since they are much larger birds, they execute all maneuvers in a more protracted manner. Time seems to have been suspended for the bird. Swallow-taileds commonly hunt lower than the Mississippi Kite, often just over the treetops.

Historically, the Swallow-tailed occurred north to the Great Lakes, but its breeding range is now confined to the southeastern coastal plains of South Carolina, Georgia, and Florida. The birds withdraw to South America in winter months, probably crossing the Straits of Florida to Cuba and then flying from island to island until they arrive on the continent. A very few follow a land route along the Texas coast each year. Large migratory flocks occur. Swallow-taileds are early spring migrants, arriving in late February and early March in South Florida. They depart in August and early September for their wintering quarters.

The Swallow-tailed Kite is as large as an Osprey and about twice the size of a Mississippi Kite. The bird is almost unmistakable, with its striking black-and-white patterning and long, deeply forked tail. Juveniles resemble adults but have streaking on the breast and shorter, less distinctive, and deeply forked tails.

The Swallow-tailed often eats reptiles and amphibians, but it is at its graceful best when catching insects over the hummocks and glades of South Florida. The bird is quite social and (except when out of its normal range) is rarely seen alone, even during the nesting season.

In part due to its considerable powers of flight, the Swallow-tailed Kite (like the Mississippi Kite) has a propensity for appearing far out of its normal range, and it has appeared at most major spring hawk-watch sites. It is seen annually as far north as New Jersey. Most of the overshoots are encountered between mid-April and late May.

IDENTIFICATION. This is a large, distinctive raptor — a bird that virtually anyone could identify the first time out. To belabor its identifying characteristics would be a cruel disservice to students of raptor identification and to the bird. If it is seen clearly, a Swallow-tailed Kite should be instantly identifiable at any distance.

Distance is, of course, the giant equalizer, and enough of it will cause even something as obvious as a Swallow-tailed Kite to be

American Swallow-tailed Kite, underside.

American Swallow-tailed Kite, upperside.

confused with several other species. We discuss this problem in connection with telling the kites apart.

Black-shouldered Kite

The Black-shouldered Kite is a member of a widespread genus (*Elanus*), a group with a worldwide distribution whose members are currently considered conspecific. Until 1983, the North American representative of the genus was considered a separate species bearing the scientific name *Elanus leucurus* and called White-tailed Kite. Despite profound morphological differences (the European and African subspecies is considerably broader-winged and shorter-tailed), the birds are now considered to be one species.

Immature Black-shouldered Kite hovering.

The Black-shouldered Kite has had mixed fortune in North America. It was once found nesting in the Carolinas and Florida but is now confined largely to Texas and the Pacific Coast from Baja to Oregon. Over the past decade, its range has been expanding and the population increasing.

Although the bird is considered by most authorities to be non-migratory, it does wander, to a degree, in spring and fall. It habitually appears in areas of the Southwest that lie beyond its nesting range. It is again nesting in Florida and a vagrant to South Carolina. There have been recent confirmed sightings in New York and New England. The bird's propensity for wandering warrants its inclusion in this book.

The Black-shouldered Kite's preferred terrain is open country — pastures and grasslands, marshes, and alfalfa fields. It has recently begun using the grassy center or median strip and shoulders of busy interstate highways. Protected from humans by the

Adult Black-shouldered Kite going away.

Black-shouldered Kite, underside.
  (A) Adult
  (B) Immature
Slim and long-winged, with very narrow tail; wings never quite straight, even when soaring as in (B). More likely to be mistaken for a gull than for another raptor. Immatures differ from adults in having buffy streaked breast band and dusky spot at the tip of each tail feather.

high fences that border freeways (and protected also by dangerous traffic patterns), the bird is thriving in long, man-made strips of perfect habitat along California highways.

The behavior of the Black-shouldered Kite sets it apart from the other North American kites. The others described here hunt by coursing the sky, but this bird commonly hovers in a distinctive manner or hunts from a perch. Wing beats are slow and almost floppy. When prey is sighted, the bird lifts its wings high over its body and simply collapses atop its food, usually a small

Black-shouldered Kite, upperside. Immature (illustrated) has dusky tail tip, buffy wash on crown, brown spotting on back, and buffy tips on wing coverts; adults are gray, lacking all these markings. Black shoulder patches present in all plumages. In known pairs females can be identified by slightly grayer shoulder patches.

rodent (the bird's specialty). Insects and occasionally reptiles and amphibians round out the diet.

Like other kites, the Black-shouldereds are quite social and form feeding flocks. They are also crepuscular in their habits, hunting actively at dawn and dusk. They spend midday on a perch, yet at some point in good weather they often go aloft to cavort in the typical manner of a kite.

IDENTIFICATION. The Black-shouldered Kite is a medium-sized raptor proportionately similar to a Mississippi Kite but slightly larger. Adults are pale gray above and white below, with obvious black patches on the shoulders (lesser and median secondary coverts), visible whether the bird is perched or in flight. Immatures have a ruddy-colored breast, a brown back, and a conspicuous narrow band at the end of the tail.

The falconlike wings are usually held above the horizontal in a dihedral. When coursing over a field, the bird usually turns its head downward; the head moves from side to side as the bird searches for prey below.

The Black-shouldered Kite hover-hunts habitually and suggests an oversized American Kestrel. But at virtually any distance, plumage is the distinguishing characteristic. Any white Kestrel (sic) with black shoulders, is not.

Telling Kites Apart

Kites have qualities that also belong to other types of birds. They are distinctly falconlike in shape. Their stiff, languid flight and slim, pointed wings recall the family Laridae. In some circumstances they may even be readily mistaken for such improbable look-alikes as a Ferruginous Hawk or a Northern Harrier. A classic case in point is the problem of differentiating immature Mississippi Kites from immature Peregrine Falcons.

The average Peregrine, with its 40-inch wingspan, is considerably larger than a Mississippi Kite, which has a 35-inch wingspan. But the smaller tiercel Peregrine causes confusion not only because of its size but because its proportions are slimmer and more kitelike than those of the female Peregrine.

Adult kites are always readily distinguishable from Peregrines. The light gray or white head, the rich, dark gray underparts, and particularly the large white upperwing patch (secondaries) make the bird virtually unmistakable. (Note: the white wing patch is larger and whiter, in good light, than field guides indicate.) Worth noting, too, is the fact that the back of an adult Mississippi Kite is darker than that of an adult *tundrius* Peregrine, which has a pale blue-gray back.

Caution: a light or white head does not automatically make a distant falconlike bird a kite. Immature tundra Peregrines (those most commonly seen in migration) have a pale cap which makes the birds look blond or white-headed.

Immature and subadult kites are not nearly as distinctive or readily identifiable as adults. First-year birds are somewhat variable, ranging from sandy tan (with darker streakings) to dark chocolate brown all over with little streaking. Subadults may be all dark gray or brownish gray throughout, with no streaking on the underparts (they will sometimes show pale, bleached spots on the gray to gray-brown underparts). These dark immature Mississippi Kites are easily confused with Peregrines.

When distance obscures the face pattern of an immature Peregrine, an immature kite and an immature Peregrine will appear exactly the same color. At close range the transparent white barring of an immature kite's tail is diagnostic (a Peregrine Falcon's tail may be barred, but the dark markings appear on a brown background, so that they are hard to see).

The Mississippi Kite has an extremely short anterior primary. Although this may sound like a fine point, it is actually a very easy characteristic to see. The outer flight feathers of a Peregrine are more equal in length and more densely packed (so that it is difficult to see individual feathers).

Mississippi Kites and Peregrine Falcons differ in shape primarily in the tail. The Mississippi Kite's tail is proportionately longer than a Peregrine's. In addition the tail splays out toward the tip — a dead giveaway. The tail of a Peregrine tapers toward the tip.

The tail is also more squared off on the kite. The tip stops abruptly in a sharp, flat cut. The tail of a Peregrine is rounded and is commonly notched when folded. Immature Peregrines also boast a broad, buffy terminal band (a feature lacking on kites). Finally, the tail of a Mississippi Kite is almost always in constant motion, twisting and turning like a long-bladed leaf in the wind.

Behavior probably provides the best clue to the identity of a distant falcon or kite. Most apparent is the difference in the wing beats of the two birds. The wing beat of the Mississippi Kite is stiff, languid, and somewhat dainty. The wing beat of a Peregrine is powerful, rapid, and fluid — the entire wing ripples with each stroke.

The Peregrine flaps much more than the Mississippi Kite. In this respect, the kite is much like a vulture; it flaps only when all else fails. In addition, the kite rarely soars (preferring to sail or glide). Peregrines frequently soar. It is fortunate that kites tend *not* to soar because the two birds look virtually identical when they are soaring. If they are overhead, the subtle difference in the length of the outermost flight feather may easily be noted. The translucent bars on the tail of an immature Mississippi Kite are distinctive. When the tail is fully fanned, its distinctive shape loses its impact. When the soaring Peregrine is viewed at a distance (wing-on), its wings are slightly upswept at the tip; the Mississippi Kite's wings will look somewhat droopy or downcurved.

It is worth noting that wing position is also helpful when the bird is sailing or gliding. Peregrines show an abrupt upward tilt at midwing, at the joint. The hand rises and straightens as the bird maneuvers (almost like the flaps on the wing of a plane). The wings of a Mississippi Kite curve down gently, smoothly, throughout their length.

The Swallow-tailed Kite could probably be confused only with a distant Osprey or an adult male Northern Harrier. The Osprey and the Swallow-tailed Kite both have dark upperparts, white underparts, swept-back wings, and a glide with downcurved wings. But the Swallow-tailed Kite has a curve throughout the length of its wing, both in ventral profile and head-on, and never shows the angular wing shape of an Osprey. In addition, as noted above, the tail is distinctive and the back is blue-black in good light.

The only other bird with which a Swallow-tailed Kite might possibly be confused is not a raptor but the Magnificent Frigatebird (*Fregata magnificens*). The immature Frigatebird does have a white head and underparts (like the kite) but lacks the kite's white wing linings. In range these two birds overlap in Florida, and awareness of this fact is probably the best defense against confusing the two species.

With its deep, stiff, and very lazy wing beat the Swallow-tailed Kite seems to do everything in slow motion. This characteristic is so distinctive, so indicative of the bird, that, once seen, it will inevitably always call to mind the Swallow-tailed Kite.

The Black-shouldered Kite shares several characteristics with other North American raptors but is too dissimilar to the American Kestrel, the Northern Harrier, or the Ferruginous Hawk to be confused with them.

The Black-shouldered Kite most closely resembles the adult

Ring-billed Gull (*Larus delawarensis*) and the Mew Gull (*Larus canus*). The two gull species are roughly the same size as the kite and are gray above and white below, with long, tapered wings that are dark at the tips. But gulls have very large heads that are roughly as long as the tail. Kites are very small-headed birds that have very long tails. Gulls also have a downward crook in the wings. Black-shouldered Kites fly with a dihedral. And although gulls can and do hover, they do so only with obvious effort. Hovering is as natural as flight to a Black-shouldered Kite.

The Northern Harrier

The Great Fooler

SPECIES

Circus cyaneus

A slim, graceful raptor of open areas, the Northern Harrier is North America's sole representative of a genus whose nine species claim territory on every continent except Antarctica. Perhaps because it is common throughout much of its North American range and conspicuous in open haunts (and perhaps, too, because its characteristic low, cruising hunting flight appears lazy to the human eye), the bird is underrated. The Harrier is nevertheless an admirably versatile, dogged, and enigmatic raptor. If you were to study the many facets of raptordom — migration, breeding strategy, venatic versatility, and the like — and to trace the lines of evolutionary development to their culmination, your search would probably end with the underrated Harrier.

As a hunter, the Harrier is a master of the subtle art of sneaking up from behind; its standard mode of hunting seems to echo the old adage "nothing ventured, nothing gained." A low, cruising flight is punctuated at intervals by pull-ups, wing-overs, and drop-pounces — just the strategy needed to trap a tide-flushed meadow vole or a luckless Red-winged Blackbird.

The Harrier can take flying songbirds in the manner of a Cooper's Hawk. It can perch-hunt like a Kestrel, stoop like a Red-tailed Hawk, hover-hunt like a Rough-legged Hawk, chase prey through dense brush on foot like a Goshawk, pirate prey from an overloaded Peregrine, and make short work of a muskrat carcass discarded by some trapper. In short, if there is a meal to be had, the Harrier will have it.

In winter, the birds often roost communally on the ground. Individuals fan out during the day to hunt. On territory, the Har-

Adult male Northern Harrier flapping.

rier is secretive. A flushed bird will quickly abandon its ground-level nest during incubation, but if young are present, the Harrier can be a dogged defender. The male rarely visits the nest before the young are well developed. Prey carried in by the male is transferred in flight to the female, who leaves the nest in response to his calls. The female does not return to the nest site directly. She makes several false landings first to confuse any watchful predators, scavengers, or researchers.

When the male is not hunting for the female or young, he is sitting nearby as a watchful gray sentinel on a low perch. He intercepts and escorts out any high-soaring Red-tailed Hawk that enters protected airspace. Harriers often show a high degree of tolerance for nearby nesting pairs. Another bird is often allowed to hunt in close proximity to a neighbor's nest. Harriers are less patient with unattached subadults, who are harassed and driven from the area — sometimes aggressively.

In migration, Harriers are often the first birds of the day recorded on a hawk watch and just as often the last. Not surprisingly, they are crepuscular and share several convergent evolutionary traits with the owls (for example, a facial disk and a refined sense of hearing). Harriers have been seen coming in from the ocean before sunrise, hunting on moonlit nights, and, twice, migrating through the beam of the Cape May Point lighthouse after midnight.

The Harrier's migration spans the whole of autumn (July through December) and leaves just enough time for a short breather and spring rebound (February through June). Harriers will commonly migrate in weather conditions that discourage other raptors, such as blind fog, snow, sleet, freezing rain, and full-blown gales. They display little, if any, aversion to overwater migration. They have been recorded more than 50 miles off the Atlantic Coast and habitually migrate across Yakutat Bay on the Alaskan coast, a distance of 40 miles. They have also been recorded on the island of Bermuda, where Harriers are not native.

The North American breeding range of these birds encompasses approximately three-quarters of the continent, from the Arctic Ocean south to North Carolina, Texas, and southern California. During winter, the bird vacates the portion of its range that lies north of the Canadian border and Massachusetts. Arctic breeders are highly migratory; some winter as far south as Central America. But most Harriers spread out, finding suitable habitat in the southern two-thirds of the continental United States, where they occupy upland fields, freshwater and saltwater marsh, sagebrush, and farmlands — in short, any relatively open place with the promise of prey. The larger females tend to hunt broad, open areas; males commonly hunt upland borders or smaller overgrown areas.

Migration

Spring and fall migration periods are both protracted. The Harrier has the longest overall migration period of any North American raptor. In spring, adult males begin to pass through coastal and interior sites in late February and early March. Females follow in mid-March through April, and subadults through May and into early June. This staggered pattern is reversed in the fall. Immature birds can be seen passing hawk-watch sites (either as migrants or during postfledging dispersal) in mid-July through September. Females appear through October, and males are most common during November and on into early December. This general schedule is not absolute. Adult males and females can and do occur as early as late August at northeastern hawk-watch points.

Though the bird is not reluctant to cross open water, watch sites located near the coast or on the shore of the Great Lakes record greater numbers of Harriers than do those inland (on ridges). By far, the greatest recorded movements have occurred at Cape May, New Jersey, in the fall (record: 3,118, fall 1980); at Sitkagi Beach, Alaska (record: 856, April 19–May 5, 1982); and at Sandy Hook, New Jersey, in the spring (record: 525, spring 1985).

On the interior ridges, Harriers often ignore updrafts and fly wide of the ridge or high overhead. During spring migration in particular, birds seem to ignore the ridges and are often seen crossing them, heading north.

Though Harriers are commonly seen migrating alone, pairs and small groups of three to five birds are often reported, particularly when large numbers occur. The small groups usually travel in single file. It is a good practice to check first ahead of any migrating Harrier and then behind to pick up additional birds.

Identification

The Northern Harrier is a long, lean, lanky, narrow-winged, and long-tailed raptor of medium size. Females are noticeably larger and more broadly proportioned than males. Adult plumages are sexually dimorphic. Males are silver gray above and white below. Wing tips, seen from above or below, are jet black. Females are tawny above and buffy below, with brown streaking extending down the sides of the chest and flanks. Immatures of both sexes have chocolate brown backs with rusty overtones; they are rich orange to cinnamon below and show no obvious streaking. In spring, subadult males and females show a mixture of the lighter adult plumage and the darker immature plumage.

In all plumages, there is a large, conspicuous white patch on the rump. Other species of raptors have white on the proximal end of the tail (for example, the Rough-legged Hawk, Golden Eagle, Ferruginous Hawk, Swainson's Hawk, and Red-tailed Hawk), but only the Harrier has a *rump* patch.

The wings are exceedingly long and very narrow and, depending on how they are held, may appear pointed (falconlike) or

Northern Harrier, underside.
  (A) Immature
  (B) Adult male
  (C) Adult female
Shape always distinctive: long primaries; long tail; slender body; long, narrow wings; tail often held closed when soaring, and even then the bird rises faster in thermals than other raptors. Females are noticeably larger and bulkier than males. Adult males are striking, with clean white body and wing linings, gray breast, and black tips on secondaries and outer primaries. Adult females are pale buffy, with heavy spotting and streaking on the body and underwing coverts, jagged barring on flight feathers, and dark secondaries. Immature is like female but has unstreaked orange on body and underwing coverts and very dark secondaries and greater coverts, creating a dark patch on inner wing more prominent than on female.

blunt (accipiterlike). Though the bird should not pose a difficult identification problem — *nothing* looks like a Harrier except another Harrier — it is habitually mistaken for either a falcon or an accipiter by people who don't expect to see the ground-hugging Harrier high overhead.

Northern Harrier, upperside.
(A) Adult male
(B) Immature
White rump always conspicuous. Adult male is silvery gray with variable brown back and lesser coverts and with black tips on secondaries and outer primaries, as on underwing. Immature is dark brown with buffy tips on greater coverts and pale buffy bar across lesser coverts. Female is similar but paler and more spotted; flight feathers grayer and barred.

The Harrier's tail is long and narrow. It is proportionately the longest tail found on any North American raptor. When the bird is soaring, it frequently holds its tail closed, and even when the tail is fanned, it still conveys an overall impression of unusual length.

When the Harrier is soaring or gliding, it holds its wings in a bold dihedral, a field mark evident at great distances. Other birds have a dihedral, but a Harrier lifts its wings at a more acute angle than other species. The Harrier's very light wing loading causes it to rock unsteadily in a wind, and it is easily buffeted even by moderate breezes. On windless days, when the bird uses thermals for lift or exploits a weak updraft off a ridge, it will sometimes fly with its wings held flat or, more rarely, with just a hint of a downward droop. But the stiffly held, uplifted V-shaped wings are the Harrier trademark.

In migration, the course is steady and direct, quite unlike the wandering hunting flight that most observers associate with the bird. Wing beats may be steady and continuous but most often occur in a long series interspersed with slow glides (during the glide a rocking motion can often be seen). Though the Harrier is adept at soaring, it will often flap for lift even when it is riding a thermal.

The wing beat of a Harrier is loping and regular. The downward stroke is punctuated by a crisp, emphatic snap. The cadence is unique. Observers familiar with it can identify distant Harriers by this feature alone.

Seen from below, the ghostly white underparts and ink-black wing tips of an adult male are utterly distinctive. Immatures and, to a lesser degree, females, have a characteristic plumage that is only slightly less distinct. The wing linings and outer flight feathers of both females and immatures are lighter than the secondaries. As a result the wing appears light along the leading edge and dark along the trailing edge — somewhat suggesting the wing pattern of a Swainson's Hawk and very unlike that of most raptors.

Telling Harriers from the Rest

It would seem, at first glance, that the Harrier's distinctive shape and plumage should keep it from being mistaken for any other species of raptor, but for several reasons this is not the case. In fact, the opposite seems to be true. Nobody will ever know how many high-flying Harriers have been recorded as Peregrines or how many Harriers have been transformed into Cooper's Hawks by inexperienced observers — observers who could not, after convincing themselves that the bird was definitely not a Sharp-shinned Hawk, look beyond the very long, rounded tail to notice all the other traits uncharacteristic of a Cooper's Hawk.

At just about any distance this side of the limit of detection, the dihedral of a Harrier will be plainly visible unless the bird is directly overhead. This feature alone precludes confusion with falcons or accipiters, and the rocking flight eliminates from consideration all raptors but the Turkey Vulture and Swainson's Hawk.

When the bird is flapping, the slow, deep, regular, loping wing beat is wholly unlike the shallow, liquid, whipping, rapid wing movement of a Peregrine and bears little resemblance to the sputtery flap and sail of a Sharp-shinned Hawk or the quicker, arthritic flap of a Cooper's Hawk. If the bird is not flapping, just wait. It will.

Mississippi and Swallow-tailed kites are probably the only other two species that might be confused with a distant Harrier. The wing beats of a kite are stiffer, more shallow, and more hurry-up-and-wait. When a kite flaps, there is acceleration. When it glides, forward momentum drops noticeably. The Harrier seems just to keep plugging along at the same easy pace, whether it is flapping or gliding.

Harriers are mistaken for other birds chiefly when they are moving high overhead. Often observers are not aware that Harriers can fly at extreme heights (they have been recorded as high as 3,000 feet over Cape May). As a result, these observers do not even consider the Harrier a possibility when they are puzzling out an identification.

Furthermore, because the bird has two very distinct and virtually unmistakable field marks (the white rump patch and the dihedral wing shape), other excellent field marks are overlooked. Many birders who have seen numbers of Harriers can identify them consistently, providing that they see the white rump or observe the bird in flight over classic habitat, but if the standard identification marks are not evident (for example, when the Harrier flies directly overhead), these same people do not recognize the bird.

Seen from below, in length and narrowness a Harrier's wings

and tail exceed those of all other raptors. The white underparts of the adult male with the contrasting black wing tips and the inverse wing pattern of the immatures and females (light in front, dark behind) are also distinctive and helpful.

Eagles and Vultures
Big Black Birds

S P E C I E S

Turkey Vulture, *Cathartes aura*
Black Vulture, *Coragyps atratus*
Bald Eagle, *Haliaeetus leucocephalus*
Golden Eagle, *Aquila chrysaetos*

Only in a book on the flight identification of raptors could these taxonomically dissimilar species be considered candidates for a group. In the hawk-watching arena, a playing field whose boundaries extend beyond simple field identification, the birds drop their distinguishing features like so many worn flight feathers. At the point where the niceties of field identification disappear, the fundamental similarities reign: large size; overall blackness; and direct, level flight on motionless wings.

Migration

Turkey Vultures, in populations far enough north to necessitate migration south for the winter, are some of the first birds to return in the spring and some of the last birds to depart in the fall. Over much of their range, they are permanent residents, but southern roosts are augmented by northern birds, and large numbers move south into Mexico each fall. As is evident from the spring counts in Texas and at Derby Hill, New York, and from the fall counts at Cape May, New Jersey, at least parts of the population are quite migratory.

The Black Vulture's range would have made the bird a wonderful symbol for the Confederacy. Until just recently, it occurred entirely within the South and the border states. As a breeder it is absent from New England, the plains states, the Rockies, and the

Immature Golden Eagle (*right*) with Turkey Vulture (*left*).

West Coast. It is essentially nonmigratory (though spring counts in Texas give evidence to the contrary). Stray birds overshoot their known breeding range each spring. Look for them in the Northeast from March through May.

Bald Eagle migration looks different, depending on where you watch. On the interior ridges of the Northeast, two separate movements in the spring and fall are sometimes thought to reflect the movements of two different subspecies. A number of Bald Eagles pass ridge watch sites during late August and early to mid-September. These may be southern birds returning to breeding territories in Florida after a summer in the cooler north. In November and early December, more Bald Eagles pass through, perhaps northern birds moving out ahead of the freeze.

A two-stage migration also occurs in the spring. At Derby Hill, a push, consisting largely of adults, occurs during late March, and a second migration, consisting chiefly of immatures, occurs in mid to late April.

A staggered migration timetable is not evident on the Atlantic Coast. Sightings at Cape May, New Jersey, occur randomly throughout the year. To a large degree the reason is that the birds seen at the Cape are virtually all immatures, which are not bound by territories. Immature eagles are great wanderers and move from one opportune food source to another. Two or three days of northwesterly winds are likely to produce an immature Bald Eagle at Cape May in any month of the year.

Golden Eagle migration is more straightforward. Even during migration, the birds favor the interior ridges. In the East, between 40 and 60 birds a year are seen at watch points along the Kittatinny Ridge in Pennsylvania — and progressively more birds are seen the farther west observations are conducted. Golden Eagles seen before October are exceptional; peak movements occur between the end of October and the first week of November. The same timetable applies to coastal areas, but the numbers are just a fraction of ridge totals (the average is five to ten birds a year at Cape May).

In the West, a large movement of Golden Eagles occurs in the Rockies and in associated western ranges during September and October, earlier than the migration in the East. Because of the abundance of ridges that run along a north-south axis, western eagle migration is diffuse; no single migratory vantage point is known to be best. Counts at Bridger Mountain, Montana, however, from September 24 to October 6, 1979 (Tilly), and periodically in 1980, listed totals of 342 and 211 Golden Eagles, respectively, and indicate a very sizable migration. Immature birds migrate first; adults follow.

Spring migration along the southern shore of the Great Lakes occurs in two stages. Adults move through between middle and late March; immatures appear from mid-April to about the first of May.

Identification

This section might more appropriately be entitled "How to Turn a Distant Vulture into an Eagle," because, in most places where avid hawk watchers congregate, eagles are the sought-after bird. Vultures (and most often the Turkey Vulture) just camouflage the real article.

Plumage and size are key considerations in differentiating the several big black birds. These birds contrast starkly with other raptors, arouse extra interest, and merit long, hard scrutiny. Though size is rarely in itself a useful field mark, it relates closely to a bird's manner of flight. Large birds appear steady or ponderous or stately. Moreover, all except one of the several big black birds have bold silver or white diagnostic marks, so that each may be considered distinctive.

The Generic Big Black Bird

Each of the birds in question is a large to massive raptor with blunt and broadly proportioned wings. The size manifests itself in the slower, more deliberate manner of flight and a scant use of wing beats. The bird appears dark, almost black. In many cases, large, clean, white or dirty white patches are found on the wings (particularly the underwings), on the tail, and, in the case of one species, on the head and body.

Because of its size, the bird can be detected at greater distances than smaller, paler species.

Vultures

The North American vultures are masters of two disciplines: soaring and sanitation. Both birds are large; both are dark, bordering on black; and both feed principally on carrion (although both species are capable of killing small, weak or sickly animals).

Black and Turkey vultures have bare, unfeathered heads — an adaptive trait that they share with several Old World vultures. This adaptation is helpful when the bird feeds on carrion. Simply stated, a naked head plunged deep into the interior of a carcass

Three Turkey Vultures and one Black Vulture (*second from right*).

will not accumulate as much gore as a well-feathered one would.

The Turkey Vulture occurs throughout the United States and southern Canada. Northern birds vacate the high-latitude portions of their range in winter and gather in large, communal roosts from northern New Jersey south to Central America. Black Vultures are considered nonmigratory, though observations in southeastern Texas and Panama in the spring indicate that they are otherwise. Like Turkey Vultures, Black Vultures assemble in roosts during the winter, sometimes with Turkey Vultures but more often not. Both species are extending their ranges northward. Prospecting Turkey Vultures have been recorded in Alaska, and Black Vultures have been sighted in the spring on the south shore of Lake Ontario.

Vulture species are highly gregarious. The birds roost together, soar together, and, if a particular carcass is large enough, feed together. Even during the breeding season, birds will often nest in close proximity to a winter roost and will occasionally return to the roost for the night.

The populations of both species appear stable. Distribution within the ranges fluctuates, according to the season and depending on land use practices. In North America, both species are common on farmland and rangeland but are less likely to occur in more developed areas: suburban sanitation measures leave scavengers slim pickings. In the tropics and the Third World countries of South and Central America, where sanitation technology has not reached state-of-the-art levels, Black and Turkey vultures are common town and city dwellers.

The vultures lack the fierce, predatory demeanor that we seem to expect in birds of prey, and their feeding habits do little to enhance their image. Nevertheless, they are master soarers, able to tease lift from thin air when other soaring birds can only sit and watch. Few creatures can ride the wind as well as a vulture.

IDENTIFICATION: TURKEY VULTURE. The Turkey Vulture is a large raptor nearly as big as an eagle. The sexes are similar. From a distance, the bird appears uniformly dark and nearly black except for the flight feathers. Seen from below, the entire outer and

Turkey Vulture, underside. Long broad wings held in pronounced dihedral; broad, fingered wing tips; fairly long tail; tiny head. Black body and underwing coverts contrast with silvery flight feathers.

trailing edge of the wing shines silver, contrasting starkly with all-black underparts and a gray tail. Adults and immatures differ only in head color. Adults have naked red heads and bright yellow bills; immatures have dull, unfeathered gray heads and gray bills (as do Black Vultures). In other words, a bird that doesn't have a red head may still be a Turkey Vulture.

Subadult birds have red heads but lack the bright yellow bill of adults.

The wings are long, broad, and planklike. The feathers at the wing tips are deeply slotted, so that they resemble widely spread

Turkey Vulture, upperside. All feathers brownish black; worn coverts (conspicuously brownish and contrasting with darker flight feathers and newer coverts) are also visible at rest and can be helpful in separating perched vultures; Black Vulture is plain coal black.

fingers. The tail is broad and is commonly not fanned as are those of most soaring raptors. The head is diminutive — ridiculously small — and its size is accentuated by the full, broad, heavily feathered neck. Turkey Vultures give the impression, in flight, of having a long tail and no head.

The wings are characteristically held sharply uplifted in a bold dihedral that gives them a V-shape. Several other species of raptors hold their wings this way, including the Golden Eagle, the Northern Harrier, the Rough-legged Hawk, the Red-tailed Hawk, Swainson's Hawk, the Ferruginous Hawk, and the Zone-tailed Hawk. Most of these species do not hold their wings as sharply upturned as the Turkey Vulture. Only the Golden Eagle, the dark phases of the several buteos mentioned, and the Zone-tailed Hawk (in the Southwest) resemble a Turkey Vulture enough to cause confusion. With the exception of the Zone-tailed Hawk, only the Turkey Vulture habitually rocks in flight, unsteadily, like a tightrope walker, arms extended to maintain balance. This airborne balancing act is apparent even in a light to moderate breeze. Harriers often rock in flight, but the motion is more suggestive of a ship riding a swell (in light winds), and Harriers are much smaller, slimmer-winged birds and never look black.

The rocking motion alternately exposes and hides the silvery underwings, making them seem at a distance to flash, like a mirror catching the sun, as the bird rocks in flight or wheels in a thermal.

Once airborne, Turkey Vultures rarely need to flap. When they do, the wing beat is heavy and deep — quite eaglelike. Turkey Vultures also have the curious habit of drooping their wing tips and quickly straightening them in a sort of mock-flap. The arm remains rigid; the hands simply wilt and then snap back. No other species of raptor manifests this behavior, and Turkey Vultures do so habitually.

The Golden Eagle is probably the bird most likely to be confused with a Turkey Vulture. Golden Eagles are large, dark, long-tailed, and proportionately short-headed. Golden Eagles also fly with their wings in a dihedral. But Golden Eagles *do not rock in flight*. The flight of an eagle is steady.

IDENTIFICATION: BLACK VULTURE. The Black Vulture bears a superficial resemblance to a Turkey Vulture, but at a distance it is far more likely to be mistaken for an eagle. Like other species in this grouping, the Black Vulture has uniformly dark, almost black plumage except for a naked gray head and (to the delight of hawk

Black Vulture, head-on.

Black Vulture, underside. Short and squat. Wings and tail much shorter than on Turkey Vulture; shape more angular, head rounder, bill thinner. Uniformly coal black except for six silvery outer primaries.

watchers everywhere) bold, white (not silver) patches on both wing tips that are visible from above and below. Except in Florida and Texas, where the Crested Caracara also occurs, a large, black raptor with obvious white wing tips is a Black Vulture. The plumage does not vary with age or sex.

Black Vultures are the smallest member of this grouping. They are a little more than two-thirds as large as a Turkey Vulture and about half the size of either species of eagle. The wings are short, broad, and stocky. The tail is ridiculously short, stubby, and usually broadly fanned. The outer tail feathers nearly touch the trailing edge of the wing. The feet can occasionally be seen trailing behind the tail, but this characteristic is not a dependable field mark. The naked head protrudes no more than the head of a Tur-

Black Vulture, upperside. Uniform black except for white shafts of outer six primaries; compare browner Turkey Vulture.

key Vulture, but because of the Black Vulture's general stockiness, it appears larger or is, at least, more prominent. In flight a Black Vulture looks like a stocky, heavy-necked, broad-winged eagle of questionable lineage.

A Black Vulture's wings are stiff and flat and rarely show any hint of a dihedral. Confusion with a Turkey Vulture is not very likely. From a distance, because of the flatness of the wings, the broad proportions of the body, and the stiff flight, Black Vultures are far more likely to be confused with eagles.

In flight, Black Vultures lack the easy grace of a Turkey Vulture or the steady stateliness of an eagle. The movements seem stiff and awkward. The wings are held tensely parallel to the body; the bird holds itself aloft in a fashion that brings to mind the image of someone riding a bicycle for the first time. A Black Vulture flaps a good deal more than a Turkey Vulture. The quick, choppy series of flaps appears frantic. Black Vultures do not rock in flight, and they do not show a dihedral. They are not difficult to identify at a reasonable distance.

Eagles

With the loss of California's wild condors, the Bald and Golden eagles are the largest birds of prey in North America. They have, in addition, at least one singular characteristic. It has been observed that most birds of prey look back over their shoulders before striking prey (or shortly thereafter); predation is after all a two-edged sword. All hawks seem to have this habit, from the smallest Kestrel to the largest Ferruginous — but not the eagles.

Eagles' fortunes in human history have been changeable. The birds have been endowed with some of the traits that rank most highly in human esteem: courage, strength, and dignity. Eagles have also been called lazy and thieving and have been charged with eating the hearts of newborn lambs and with stealing children from cribs. Eagles have ridden on the flagstaffs of conquering armies, have rested on the gloved fists of emperors, have suffered the vengeance of ranchmen for depredation of sheep.

Apart from their encounters with humans, however, North America's two resident eagles are superbly refined predators with habits more dissimilar than alike. Neither species fares well (or lives long) in the world of man's making, though both are quick to use man's modifications to advantage. Bald Eagles will gather below hydroelectric stations to harvest the bounty of turbine-killed fish, and in the tree-poor West, Golden Eagles habitually use telephone poles as hunting perches.

But eagles need a measure of solitude and space to accommodate their size. We humans seem to be ambivalent. On the one hand we pass laws to protect the birds; on the other we undermine their existence by the spread of our own species, as if to say that eagles shouldn't stand in the way of growth and development just because they are big and grand.

Four species of eagles representing two genera have been recorded in North America, but only the Golden Eagle and the Bald Eagle can be described as residents. The White-tailed Eagle (*Haliaeetus albicilla*), with populations in Greenland and Asia, was recorded in Massachusetts on November 14, 1914, bred once on

Cumberland Sound on the western shore of the Davis Strait in 1879, and has been incidental on the Aleutian chain and outlying islands of the Alaskan coast. In 1982, a pair was confirmed to be breeding on Attu Island — an island that is technically part of North America, although it would seem to be in Asia. In 1986, only one adult and one nonbreeding immature were present.

The Steller's Sea Eagle (*Haliaeetus pelagicus*) is a resident of northeastern Asia; it winters south to Japan and occasionally wanders to the Aleutians and to Kodiak Island.

Bald Eagle. The Bald Eagle is the more widespread of our two native eagles. Unlike the Golden, which occurs in Europe and Asia, the Bald Eagle is wholly confined to North America. Its range, broadly speaking, covers all of North America south of the tree line. Actually, the bird is uncommon away from coastal areas,

Adult Bald Eagle turning away.

large inland lakes, or rivers, although some birds winter on the western plateau, where they feed, to a large extent, on jackrabbits.

The bird is commonly called a fish-eating eagle, a description which is neither wholly accurate nor fair because the bird is an accomplished and versatile hunter — more versatile than the Golden Eagle. Fish — captured as prey, taken as carrion, or pirated from an Osprey (or from a smaller or younger eagle) — does indeed constitute a large part of the Bald Eagle's diet. But water-fowl concentrations attract eagles, and Balds hunt flocks of puddle ducks and snow geese with a combination of herding tactics and tail-chases. Crippled birds are probably most likely to be taken. But Bald Eagles hunting Black Ducks in coastal marshes appear to have little trouble closing on flocks that lift off ahead of them and in such cases take any bird they choose. The Bald Eagle is probably more accurately described as a forager than as a fish eater.

Perch-hunting is a common practice (in contrast, the Golden Eagle uses search-and-soar tactics). Partly for this reason, Bald Eagles do a great deal of sitting and will often not move from a perch for hours (and sometimes not for a whole day). Such energy conservation promotes survival, and the bird's relative inactivity also demonstrates its ability to locate and capture food at need.

IDENTIFICATION. The Bald Eagle is a massive, long-winged, darkly plumaged raptor larger than any buteo or vulture. Specimens vary considerably in size, but even the smallest Bald Eagle will seem immense. Adults, birds aged four years or older, have the well-known, virtually unmistakable gleaming white heads and tails. Young birds lack these features and are easily confused with the Golden Eagle, which they resemble. At sufficiently great distances they may also be confused with vultures and with some buteos.

Young birds are dark chocolate brown and appear almost black at a distance. The body, wings, and tail are often speckled or patterned with dirty white feathering. In quantity and distribution this white mottling varies greatly and is related to age. On most of the young birds that are seen (first-year or hatching-year birds), the white mottling is restricted to the underwing linings and appears as a broad, white line along the leading edge of the wing. The axillars (wing pits), too, are often very white. The flight feathers and body are dark or sparsely speckled with white.

Second- and third-year eagles may have lavish amounts of white scattered on the underwings and back but particularly on the belly. From a distance, heavily mottled birds may appear creamy

Bald Eagle, underside.
  (A) First year
  (B) Adult
Wing shape slightly less buteo-like than on Golden Eagle but very similar; head larger, tail slightly shorter. Adults have thinner, straighter wings than immatures. Adult unmistakable; immatures extremely variable (see pp. 148, 149). Individual illustrated is a more or less typical first-year bird, with dark body and patches of white on underwing coverts, primarily on axillaries and along median coverts.

or even golden below (distance blends the dark brown feathers with the white ones). On a few birds, the back and upper wings may also be tawny. Third-year birds begin to develop the white head and white tail of adults. The tail commonly has a narrow dark trim along the tip.

Immature Bald Eagles display an almost infinite variety of plumage combinations (unlike the immature Golden Eagle, whose white areas are restricted to the tail and to the base of the flight feathers). Any immature eagle with lavish amounts of white

A

B

C

Bald Eagle, upperside.
  (A) Adult
  (B) White extreme, third year
  (C) First year
Progression of plumages resembles that on underside (see p. 148); first-year birds all dark above, with pale base of tail; light covert bars appear with wear. All white-bellied birds (B) have a triangular white patch on the upper back; this individual (also shown in the next figure) is the white extreme. Adults are very dark brown except for white primary shafts and white head, tail, and rump.

on the back, belly, and particularly the underwing linings may safely be called Bald.

The tail of most immatures is dark for two-thirds to three-quarters of its length; white appears only near the base. The line of demarcation between the white base of the tail and darker portions is not sharply defined. More developed (second- and third-year birds) often show a dark, well-defined terminal band almost identical to that found on immature Golden Eagles.

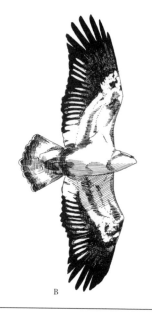

A   B

Bald Eagles of different ages.
  (A) Four-year-old
  (B) Three-year-old, white extreme
  (C) Two-year-old, typical
  (D) One-year-old, dark extreme
Dark-bellied first-year bird (D) shown here is as dark as Bald Eagles get, in
the plumage most difficult to distinguish from Golden Eagle. By age two,
birds are white-bellied, as in (C), and some become mostly white, as in (B),
suggesting Osprey, before molting to dark-bodied adult-type plumage by
fourth year. Bird (A) is adultlike, with narrow, straight-edged wings and all-
dark body but retains dark line through eye and dark tip on tail.

The head of a Bald Eagle is massive, the bill likewise. On adult
birds, the head and tail are of almost equal length. Young birds
have longer tails. Nevertheless, even young Bald Eagles appear
big-headed (the head seems to be two-thirds to one-half the
length of the tail). When the bird is in flight, there seems to be as
much head in front of a Bald Eagle's wings as there is tail behind.
Golden Eagles have a tail three times as long as the head.

C   D

In a soar, the wings of a Bald Eagle appear incredibly long and uniformly wide throughout their length, without any obvious bulging or tapering. Adult birds have narrow, planklike wings — so narrow that they seem to defy physics. Immatures have broader, heavier wings. The tips are wide, and the outer flight feathers are deeply slotted.

When soaring, the bird holds its wings at a right angle to the body and straight out. The wings are flat throughout their length or in very calm conditions may droop moderately along their length as an Osprey's wings do.

The flight is steady, stately, deliberate, and even-keeled, without any suggestion of stiffness. The wings seem to move or flex, and the body appears to have been suspended from them. The wing beat is slow, ponderous, and somewhat stiff and describes a deep arc, with the wings raised higher on the upstroke. The bird may flap continuously — or it may never flap at all.

Adult (*left*) and immature (*right*) Golden Eagles.

Golden Eagle. If the Bald Eagle is a forager, the Golden is a hunter. Though less widespread geographically, it is by and large the more common and more evenly distributed of the two species over most of its range. Goldens are common throughout much of the West and are almost abundant in arctic regions west of Hudson Bay, where they are the dominant cliff-nesting raptor. The eastern population is limited to scattered pairs in Maine and in remote areas of Canada, including a small population in northern Labrador, but lacks the numbers found west of Hudson Bay.

Goldens do not often choose flat land (though a few birds winter each year on coastal marshes). They prefer terrain at odds with the horizon. Though they are not averse to water, they are not particularly drawn to it, in striking contrast to the Bald Eagle. If the Bald Eagle is a bird of the coast and rivers, the Golden is a confirmed inlander, a bird of dry and often water-parched re-

Golden Eagle soaring.

gions. Its prey tends to be predominantly mammals — ground squirrels, marmots, jackrabbits, foxes, and even an occasional antelope or lamb. Goldens also take waterfowl and wading birds (to the size of Canada Geese, Great Blue Herons, and cranes) and do not shun carrion (as the number of eagles poisoned by strychnine-laced carcasses indicates).

Goldens hunt from aloft more often than from a perch. Prey is spotted as the bird soars high overhead and is taken by a long, plummeting stoop. Birds in hilly country also use the strategy of hugging the contours of ridges and ravines, using terrain to shield their approach, and fully exploiting the element of surprise.

IDENTIFICATION. Golden Eagles are large and dark, in appearance and shape resembling immature Bald Eagles. The adult's body is dark brown, often with a trace of white feathering at the base of the tail. The crown and nape on both adults and immatures are blond or pale gold. On some individuals, the golden hackles can be so pronounced that, from a distance, the bird appears white-headed; more than one Golden Eagle has been pronounced an adult Bald Eagle for this reason.

Immature Golden Eagles have dark bodies, like adults, but boast brilliant white patches on the wings and a white tail broadly edged with a dark terminal band. The white wing patches may be very large and obvious (visible from above as well as below), or they may be small and visible only from below (and in adults, they are of course absent). Occasionally, particularly in the more advanced stages of juvenile plumage, the white in the wing appears as a thin white line highlighting the base of the primaries and secondaries and *running along the length of the wing*. The immature Bald Eagle's line of white runs along the wing on the underwing linings, not on the flight feathers. The areas are adjacent. The distinction is fine, but there is no overlap. Only rarely will a young Golden Eagle have any white speckling on the wing coverts or the body. Except for the white in the flight feathers (and the tail), the underparts are uniformly dark.

The tarsus on a Golden Eagle is feathered, and on a Bald Eagle

Golden Eagle, underside.
  (A) Immature
  (B) Adult
  (C) Immature
Compare with Bald Eagle. Note smaller head, longer tail, slightly more
buteo-like shape. As in Bald Eagle, immatures are broader-winged and
longer-tailed than adults. Golden hackles are present in all plumages. Typical
first-year birds have large white patches at base of primaries and base of tail;
white diminishes with age, but some adults retain white at base of tail; and
some first-year birds lack white wing patches. Note that bases of all body
feathers are white, and molt or misplaced feathers can leave white patches, as
on (C); compare with Bald Eagle, especially the dark one-year-old on p. 149.
Easily distinguished from dark-phase buteos by size and dark flight feathers.

it is bare. This point, stressed in some field guides, is functionally
useless for flight identification, since the tarsus will not be visible.
    The wings are long, broad, and roughly similar to those of a
Bald Eagle, but the wings indent slightly along the trailing edge
where they join the body, and the secondaries bulge outward.

Golden Eagle, upperside.
 (A) Immature
 (B) Adult
Golden hackles are conspicuous in all plumages. Immature shows small or no
white patches on wings, bright white base of tail, rich brown back and wing
coverts. Adult has dark tail with pale gray base, primaries and secondaries
gray with dark barring. Old and worn coverts produce light patches and bars
on wings.

This bulge gives the wing more curvature, the hint of a buteo-like
S-shape along the trailing edge, in contrast to the more planklike
look of a Bald Eagle's wing.

The head is small, the bill likewise. The tail by comparison is
quite long. In general the head of a Golden Eagle is only about
one-third the length of the tail — obviously shorter and noticeably smaller than the massive head of a Bald Eagle.

Viewed as a whole, a Golden Eagle, with its long, broad,
shapely wings, its small head, and its longer tail, greatly resembles
an overgrown, dark buteo — as the Bald Eagle almost never does.

When the bird is soaring or gliding, the wings are held flat or
in a moderate dihedral (most of the upward curvature beginning

Immature Golden Eagle (*right*) with immature Bald Eagle (*left*), soaring and turning away. Note slight dihedral of Golden. Compare shapes of both upper and lower wing tips. Bald is more angular, pointed; Golden is rounded, buteo-like. Also compare tail length and shape, head size, wing pattern.

at the wrist). The bird can easily be mistaken for a Turkey Vulture, which also displays a dihedral, although that of the Turkey Vulture is generally more pronounced. Curiously, the dihedral is rarely seen on the East Coast and seems to be a ridge-linked characteristic. Most Golden Eagles seen at coastal watch points fly flat-winged.

The wing beat of a Golden is similar to that of a Bald Eagle — slow, ponderous, and sparingly used. But it is not stiff and is far shallower than the deep, arcing wing beat of a Bald Eagle. You will not mistake it for anything less than the wing beat of an eagle. But the suggestion of a buteo's flight will not escape you, either.

Telling Big Black Birds Apart

When an eagle appears at the limit of conjecture, it gives the impression of being simply a big black bird. Because the bird is large and because it is black, it will be detected at greater distances than any lesser species would be. The distance will mask perception of any forward movement. The bird will seem to move with interminable slowness or not at all. Any black, immobile dot on the horizon should cause heightened interest.

Occasionally, in poor light or on an overcast day, a large Redtailed or Ferruginous Hawk may appear eagle-sized. As a rule, it

Eagles and vultures, all species soaring.
  (A) Turkey Vulture
  (B) Black Vulture
  (C) Bald Eagle
  (D) Golden Eagle
Vultures are distinguished by smaller size, bare heads, pale legs. Black
Vultures are readily distinguished by stubby wings and short tail; Turkey
Vulture very similar to Golden Eagle, but note two-toned wings and rocking
flight. Eagles are best distinguished by plumage; Golden has smaller head,
smaller bill, longer tail; wings slightly broader in secondaries, more rounded
at tip, with more buteo-like shape. Compare position of white patches on
wings.

is easier to turn Red-taileds into eagles than to turn eagles (or
vultures) into buteos.

When the bird is flapping, the slow, ponderous, deliberate cadence of an eagle's wing beat is discernible at almost impossible
distances (an immature Bald Eagle was identified at 2.6 miles
through 8× binoculars by its rhythm and manner of flight).

The flap of a Black Vulture is quick and choppy, not heavy or
deliberate. Turkey Vultures seem to flap only as a last resort and
will never do so steadily.

On set wings, either soaring or gliding, Turkey Vultures hold their wings in a dihedral and rock unsteadily; eagles do not. An eagle can maintain an even keel even under the highest winds that an observer is likely to survive. Since motion is discernible at distances that obscure all physical characteristics, it offers valuable clues to the identity of any distant dark bird. If the bird rocks in flight or flaps in a hurried motion, it isn't an eagle.

A distant Rough-legged Hawk can be mistaken for a Golden Eagle, but the shapes of the dihedrals differ. In Rough-leggeds, the uplift begins at the shoulder and levels out toward the wrist. A Golden Eagle's dihedral is level at the shoulder and rises abruptly from the wrist. A dark-phase Ferruginous Hawk, with its two white patches on the upper wings and its pale tail, most resembles an immature Golden Eagle in plumage — but just watch for a while. If the bird hovers or kites, it isn't an eagle.

Ospreys are sometimes mistaken for Bald Eagles because of their large size and because, when the bird is in a full soar, the crooked wing is not as apparent. But Ospreys have diminutive heads; in fact, at the distances that permit them to be confused with an eagle, Ospreys appear to have no head at all. Bald Eagles, remember, have massive heads.

On the other hand, on more than one occasion, Bald Eagles approaching an observer head-on have been mistaken for Ospreys. Bald Eagles can and do fly with down-drooped wings that resemble those of an Osprey. Third-year eagles sometimes have very white heads (sometimes with a dark eyestripe) and impressive amounts of white below.

When all possibilities have been evaluated and the bird is undeniably an eagle, the difficult part begins. Distinguishing eagles from eagles is far more difficult than separating eagles from birds of lesser lineage.

Large white wing patches in conjunction with a gleaming white tail and the absence of white on other parts of the body are virtually irrefutable evidence of an immature Golden Eagle. An eagle with large amounts of white over the body, particularly on the underparts, may safely be called Bald. A uniformly dark eagle that lacks any trace of white (except a modest amount on the base of the tail) is an adult Golden.

The tail itself is not a good identifying mark (and as previously noted, no one field mark is an infallible guide anywhere in hawk identification). Both Golden Eagles and advanced immature Bald Eagles may have white tails set off by a wide, sharply defined terminal band. But the location and distribution of white on the wings reliably differentiates the two immature eagles. Golden Eagles have white on the base of the flight feathers that usually takes the shape of a large white patch, visible on the underside and the upper surface of the wing. The patches grow smaller as the bird moves toward adulthood and may, in advanced subadult plumage, become a narrow white line running along the edge of the wing lining. *Note: the white is not on the wing lining*. But a *line* of white should immediately suggest a Bald Eagle. Immature Bald Eagles have white underwing linings, and the white very often takes the form of a line or bar running along the trailing edge of the wing coverts (*note: on the wing coverts, not on the flight feathers*).

Although some immature Bald Eagles have scattered white in the flight feathers, such birds have lavish amounts of white mottling all over (and are therefore unlikely to be confused with anything but an Osprey).

In poor light or at distances that make identification of a completely dark eagle uncertain (cases when an adult Golden might also seem to be a very unmarked immature Bald Eagle), the relative length of the head and tail is the best indicator. Tail length alone is not reliable because an immature Bald Eagle can have a very long tail — as long as that of a Golden Eagle. But birds with heads that are more than half the length of the tail can be called a Bald Eagle; birds with heads that are only one-third the length of the tail are Goldens.

The Osprey
Fish Hawk

SPECIES

Pandion haliaetus

The Osprey is a strikingly handsome, large raptor with its own evolutionary specialty — diving for fish. Bald Eagles can capture fish that swim close to the surface by flying low and casting their talons in a sweeping arc. But only the Osprey dives, talons first, often immersing itself completely in pursuit of prey.

A hunting Osprey will fly to a likely piece of water and will hover with a fisherman's patience until prey has been sighted. When the time is right, the bird folds up and dives, head first, with its wings swept back behind the tail. The bird adjusts the angle of the dive to compensate for the refraction in the image of the fish swimming below the surface. Just before hitting the water, the Osprey throws its feet forward in a four-cornered net of talons.

In more than half the cases, an adult Osprey will emerge with fish in tow. It will lift off with a single, powerful wing beat if the fish is small or with a series of quick, choppy flaps if it is large. Once clear of the water, the bird rises in flight, shedding water in a cloud of droplets. If the Osprey can escape the pirating attempts of gulls, Bald Eagles, Frigatebirds, other Ospreys, and even such unlikely brigands as the Red-tailed Hawk, it will take a perch on some isolated branch and feed. A migrating Osprey may be seen carrying fish past hawk-watch sites — "packing a lunch," as it is called in the hawk-watch vernacular. These watch sites are often miles from the nearest fishable body of water.

On one occasion, at Montclair Hawk Watch in New Jersey, an Osprey was reportedly seen carrying an orange — unlikely prey for a fish-eating bird (especially in a temperate zone). It was subsequently concluded that the bird had probably captured a goldfish in someone's ornamental pond.

Prey other than fish is infrequently taken. A snake swimming across the surface of a lake is fair game, and muskrat skulls have been found in Osprey nests, although perhaps the latter simply formed part of the flotsam and jetsam with which Ospreys adorn their impressive stick nests. Nest-building materials may include natural material such as wrack weed, desiccated carcasses of Great Blue Herons, and conch shells or even nylon webbing from beach

Osprey and Northern Harrier immatures gliding.
  (A) Osprey
  (B) Red-tailed Hawk (for size comparison)
  (C) Northern Harrier

Osprey with fish.

chairs, plastic garbage bags, discarded toys, and fish line and lures (which are sometimes lethal to the birds; young Ospreys have strangled or struggled to exhaustion after being enmeshed in fish line carried to the nests by adults).

The nests, made mostly of sticks and driftwood, are impressive structures. Pairs add material to them year after year until a storm destroys the structure or a supporting base collapses under the sheer weight of building material. In former times, the base was usually a strong-limbed tree near water that offered a panoramic view. A prime location also offered a nearby sentry perch for the male.

On the Atlantic Coast, Ospreys originally nested on the forested barrier islands. Early in the settlement of the coast, colonists and seamen clearcut the islands and created the dunes and bayberry thickets that we know today. Ospreys retreated to the broad marshes that lie between the beaches and the mainland. They nested in the gnarled remains of trees on cedar islands that were overlooked by lumber-hungry sea captains, whose eyes were on the European markets. The birds continued to fish offshore.

Ospreys are open to suggestion concerning their nest sites and are quick to adopt suitable man-made structures. The birds have built nests on duck blinds, outhouses, channel markers, grounded boats, and, of course, telephone poles — a preference that hasn't endeared the bird to the power companies. One colony in southern New Jersey uses the support struts for high-tension towers that cross open marsh.

The bird is a solitary nester through most of its range, and each pair inhabits its own territory at the edge of some inland lake. Sometimes, though, Ospreys nest in loose colonies. The colonies may occur when suitable and well-spaced support structures are in short supply, but even in locations where acceptable man-made platforms are plentiful, colonies persist.

Ospreys, as a single species, occur over much of the globe but most commonly in the Northern Hemisphere. In continental North America, the single subspecies (*P. h. carolinensis*) ranges north and west to coastal Alaska and east through the central Yukon to Newfoundland. Predictably, over its range the bird shies away from arid and treeless regions. Birds establish territories both in coastal areas and farther inland where forests rich in lakes and fish are found.

Migration

The Osprey is a long-distance migrant. Most birds winter well south of the Mexico border in Central America and in Chile, Argentina, and Patagonia. Many birds winter in Florida and a few do so in southern California, but these are probably permanent residents. Birds sighted elsewhere in December or January are exceptionally late stragglers.

In spring, Ospreys may reach the Middle Atlantic states by the first week in March, although most residents do not arrive until midmonth. Spring migration peaks between late April and early May. In autumn, birds begin to head south during the later part

Osprey approaching.

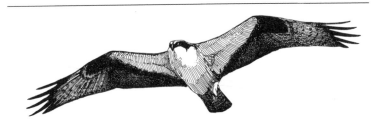

of August. The peak of the migration occurs in late September in the Northeast, and by November all but a few strays have moved through.

Large numbers of migrating Ospreys, drawn to energy-conserving updrafts, are recorded at interior watch sites. In much of the interior, the spring migration rivals the autumn migration in numbers. For most species of raptors, spring sightings are only a fraction of the numbers recorded in autumn.

Impressive numbers of Ospreys also occur at coastal hawk-watch sites in the fall and at Great Lakes sites in spring and fall — at least partly because of the availability of prey. It is a good practice upon sighting an Osprey to look ahead of the bird for another and then behind, along the same flight path. Groups of as many as 11 Ospreys have been recorded at Cape May, New Jersey, and groups of three to five are common.

Ospreys migrate later in the day than most other raptors. At Hawk Mountain, Pennsylvania, and at many other ridge sites, Ospreys have been recorded moving past the lookouts as late as observers were able to discern the shape of birds moving down-ridge.

Ospreys are graceful fliers that seem capable of finding lift when other birds cannot. In a kettle of Broad-wingeds, they will rise almost twice as fast as the milling buteos and will begin their glides much earlier. But Ospreys are content to move leisurely between thermals. Before a new thermal is reached, most of the Broad-wingeds will have passed an Osprey that preceded them at the last thermal.

Identification

An Osprey is a large raptor with distinctive black-and-white pat-terned plumage and an equally distinctive shape. It is probably the easiest North American raptor to identify and can plausibly be confused only with a Bald Eagle or a large gull. Adults and immatures are functionally similar in appearance. Upperparts are a uniform deep brown except for a white crown and forehead. A dark eyestripe separates the white crown from the white throat. Below, the body and wing linings are creamy white. The flight

Osprey, underside.
  (A) Immature
  (B) Adult
A distinctive bird, with long, crooked wings. Little plumage variation. All
have white body; alternating dark and light areas on underwing include black
carpal patch; white head with black eyestripe. Immature differs from adult in
having white-tipped secondaries and tail, more translucent inner primaries,
more neatly marked underwing, and buffy smudges on body and underwing.
Adult females tend to be more heavily marked than males, with streaked
breast band and spotted axillaries.

feathers are uniformly dark. The carpal patches are very dark, almost black, and obvious.

It could be argued that even the very basic plumage description

Osprey, upperside.
  (A) Immature
  (B) Adult
  (C) Great Black-backed Gull
Osprey is easily distinguished from gulls, particularly adult Great Black-
backed (C) by blackish rump and tail, visible at tremendous distances. Adult
(B), uniformly blackish brown above, browner on coverts when feathers are
worn. Immature (A) in fresh plumage has all feathers tipped with white.

just presented is unnecessary. Many veteran hawk watchers, people who can recognize an Osprey more than two miles away, cannot begin to recall the location of the light and dark areas on the
undersurface of an Osprey's wing. The markings are so unique
and so distinctive that the mere overall impression of bold patterning is sufficient.

For the purposes of aging and sexing, it can be noted that adult
males are clean-breasted and that females have varying amounts
of streaking in the form of a necklace on the upper chest. Adults
have more dark mottling on the underwing linings than immatures. Immatures have a narrow white border on the trailing edge

of the wings and the tip of the tail. Adults do not. Immatures also have pale edges on the back and scapular feathers, so that the upperparts look scaly or speckled.

In a full soar, the wings appear uncommonly long, thin, and lanky. The wings are more tapered than those of a Bald Eagle without actually being tapered. The arm is broad and full throughout its length, but the hand is long, narrow, and almost delicate. The arm and hand appear not to belong together on the same wing.

Ospreys are more commonly seen while gliding along a ridge or between thermals. In this attitude, the wing shape is so unlike that of other birds of prey that it overshadows all other field marks. The wing is sharply crooked; the elbows are thrust forward in front of the head; and the hands are swept back. With its deeply slotted flight feathers, the bird resembles a long-winged scarecrow with its arms thrown over the crossbar of a supporting post. Seen head-on, the bird holds its wings in an exaggerated, uplifted bow completely above the horizontal axis. The bird flies almost as if it were riding on the palms of its hands. An Osprey in flight, with its arms sharply uplifted, its long, narrow hands angled downward, and its long, narrow wings crooked sharply back, suggests a large, lanky dark-backed gull. This resemblance to a gull exists no matter how the bird is flying or soaring. As one veteran hawk counter at Cape May succinctly observed, "An Osprey is a hawk that looks like a gull but is not."

From almost any angle, the bird appears to have a small head — a trait accentuated by the length of the wing and the elbows thrust forward in a glide. The tail is of medium length and is broad. When the bird is seen high overhead or from the side, its head disappears. A distant Osprey seems to be all wing and tail.

The wing beat of an Osprey is stiff, almost arthritic. The motion seems centered at the elbows, and the hands don't contribute to the wing action. When the bird is flapping heavily, the body and (particularly) the head bob up and down in counterpoint to the stroke of the wing. The stiffness, the rhythm of the wing beat, and the bobbing motion suggest the movement of a figure on crutches. During migration, though, the bird uses updrafts and thermals extensively and rarely engages in more active flight.

Telling Ospreys from the Rest

An Osprey seems unlikely ever to be confused with another bird, but it is. Distance diminishes dissimilarity, and at a certain point even a bird as distinctive as an Osprey challenges the observer's identification skills.

The bird's resemblance to a gull has been mentioned. Ospreys have also frequently been confused with distant soaring eagles. Then, too, there have been occasions when inexperienced hawk watchers have construed the field marks (dark primaries and secondaries, white underwing linings, dark back, and long, slim, uplifted wings) as belonging to a Swainson's Hawk — an impressive feat. And more than one Osprey has been called a Red-tailed Hawk or a Ferruginous Hawk by an incautious observer because, when the bird was backlit by the sun, its tail assumed a distinctly reddish cast.

But at anything approaching a reasonable distance, an Osprey should be instantly recognizable. Of course, hawk watching is an art that concerns itself with identification at very unreasonable distances. Even at distances, altitudes, and light conditions that make color and patterning useless, the distinctive gull-shaped wing configuration should eliminate all other birds except a Bald Eagle or a gull (or, perhaps, a gliding Swainson's Hawk).

Bald Eagles occasionally glide or soar with their wings slightly drooped like those of an Osprey but without lifting the wings at the elbow. The wing of an Osprey juts sharply up above the horizontal axis and then turns downward. An eagle holds its wing level with the horizontal axis or shows a gentle downward droop.

Distant gulls, particularly the adult Great Black-backed Gull, can be mistaken for an Osprey, although more often when a number of gulls are near a hawk-watch site any Ospreys will be overlooked. Distant Ospreys will appear to have small heads or no heads; a distant Osprey appears to be all wing and tail. Gulls have large, conspicuous heads that extend well beyond the wings. Furthermore, Ospreys have broad wings that may *suggest* the long, slim, acute tapering of a gull's wing but do not duplicate it. An Osprey's wings are broader than a gull's, and the wing tips are either blunt or round (when the bird is soaring) or heavy and ragged-edged when it is gliding. A gull's wings are stiletto sharp; individual flight feathers are indistinguishable.

The wing beat of the larger species of gulls is methodical, languid, and shallow, with overtones of effortlessness or unmindfulness. The wing beat of an Osprey is stiff and labored and seems the product of a concerted effort. On the average, gulls flap a good deal more than do Ospreys.

At many, if not most, hawk-watch sites, gulls and Ospreys use different flight patterns. Gulls are not attracted to updrafts and will fly across the ridge; Ospreys are compulsive updraft users and will follow the contour of a ridge.

Photographs of Hawks in Flight

Immature Red-tailed Hawk. This bird is typical of the average Eastern Red-tailed. Cape May, New Jersey, August.

Immature Red-tailed Hawk, very white below. Cape May, December.

Red-tailed Hawk riding a gentle updraft, seen head-on. Note the slight dihedral (often more accentuated than it appears here). Texas, February.

Red-tailed Hawk, trimming its sails (*top left*). This view illustrates the stocky, blocky cut of a Red-tailed in an updraft. Raccoon Ridge, New Jersey, November.

Immature Red-tailed Hawk in a shallow glide (*top right*). Note the translucent *patches* (not crescents) in the wings. Cape May, November.

Adult Red-tailed Hawk, dorsal view (*bottom left*). Squaw Creek National Wildlife Refuge, Missouri, January.

Adult Western Red-tailed Hawk (*calurus*), light phase but still darker than the average Eastern Red-tailed Hawk (*bottom right*). The pale bands on the tail (absent in Eastern Red-taileds) are not readily visible in this photo. Elfrida, Arizona, February.

Western Red-tailed Hawk (*calurus*), dark phase. Immature (*above*). Adult: belly and wing linings are chocolate brown; chest is rufous (*opposite page*). Elfrida, Arizona, February.

Probably an immature Harlan's Hawk; note banded tail. Squaw Creek National Wildlife Refuge, Missouri, January.

Probably an immature Harlan's Hawk, identified on the basis of mottled chest, banded primaries, and long, narrow wings and tail (*top left and right*). Squaw Creek National Wildlife Refuge, Missouri, January.

Adult Harlan's Red-tailed Hawk, showing the black trailing edge of the wing, mottled breast, and black tip on a white, unbanded tail (*bottom left*). Manhattan, Kansas, January.

Adult Harlan's Red-tailed Hawk, light phase (*bottom right*). A very uncommon bird. Observe the classic Harlan's tail — white with dark *streaks* (not bands) and dark tip. Salt Plains National Wildlife Refuge, Oklahoma, January.

Adult Red-shouldered Hawk (*top left*). Note the translucent crescent "windows" at the tip of each wing and the "blueprint" tail pattern (white on a dark field). The overall stockiness and compactness of adult birds is plainly evident here. Cape May, November.

Adult Red-shouldered Hawk from Florida, with wings reaching forward in a full soar (*top right*). Note that this bird is much paler than northern or western birds. Everglades National Park, Florida, April.

Immature Red-shouldered Hawk (*bottom left and right*). The immatures have longer wings and longer tails than adults and are overall more accipiterlike. Notice also the rectangular cut of the wings. Cape May, October.

Soaring, adult Broad-winged Hawk (*left*). Raccoon Ridge, New Jersey, September. Photo by Frank Schleicher.

Broad-winged Hawk in a glide (*right*). Raccoon Ridge, New Jersey, September. Photo by Frank Schleicher.

Adult Broad-winged Hawk in a glide (*top left*). This bird has relatively dark plumage. Note the paring knife cut of the wings. Cape May, September.

Adult Broad-winged Hawk in a full soar in spring, showing the single broad white tail band and the clean white underwings (*top right*). Cape May, May.

Immature Broad-winged Hawk (*bottom left*). This bird has little spotting on the underparts. Note the semblance of a belly band and the width of the subterminal band. Cape May, September.

Immature Broad-winged Hawk (*bottom right*). Cape May, October.

Kettle of Broad-winged Hawks over Cape May, September (*opposite page*).

Adult Swainson's Hawk, light phase, with dark chest, dark flight feathers, and creamy white underparts (*top left*). Big Bend, Texas, April.

Subadult Swainson's Hawk (captured and aged in the hand) in a hard glide angle over Cape May, November (*top right*).

Adult Swainson's Hawk, light phase, showing the long, slim, tapered candlestick wings and the flight dihedral (*bottom*). Big Bend, Texas, April.

Swainson's Hawk, dark phase, and Broad-winged Hawks. Cape May, September.

Immature Rough-legged Hawk in a soar (*left*). Hackensack Meadows, New Jersey, February. Photo by Frank Schleicher.

Dark-phase Rough-legged Hawk (*right*). Hackensack Meadows, New Jersey, January. Photo by Frank Schleicher.

Immature Swainson's Hawk, light phase, with Turkey Vulture (*opposite page*). Matecumbe Key, Florida, November. Photo by Harry Darrow.

186

Rough-legged Hawk, light phase, in a glide (*top*). Note the black swath across the middle, the black carpal patches, and the pale chest, which denote an immature bird. Money Island, Delaware Bay, New Jersey, February.

Adult male Rough-legged Hawk, light phase, with dark chest and narrow bands on the tail (*bottom*). Tuckahoe River, New Jersey, February.

Immature Rough-legged Hawk, light phase. Cape May, December.

Adult Ferruginous Hawk, light phase, in direct flight (*opposite page, top*). This view shows clearly the dark leggings and the white upperwing patches. Cimarron National Grasslands, Kansas, January.

Adult Ferruginous Hawk, dorsal view (*opposite page, bottom*). Note the white wing patches and the rufous wash on the tail. Elfrida, Arizona, February.

Ferruginous Hawk, soaring (*top left and right*). Note the heavy body, the wedge-shaped head, and the long, tapered wings lifted in a dihedral. Muleshoe National Wildlife Refuge, Texas, February.

Immature Ferruginous Hawk (*bottom left*). Note the banded tail and flight feathers (lacking in adults) and the absence of leggings. Lake Henshaw, California, February.

Adult Ferruginous Hawk, dark phase (*bottom right*). Note the absence of a band on the tail. Elfrida, Arizona, February.

Immature Sharp-shinned Hawk in a shallow glide (*opposite page*). Raccoon Ridge, New Jersey, September. Photo by Frank Schleicher.

Immature Sharp-shinned Hawk in a glide (*above*). Raccoon Ridge, New Jersey, September. Photo by Frank Schleicher.

Adult Sharp-shinned Hawk, banking (*opposite page*). Raccoon Ridge, New Jersey, October. Photo by Frank Schleicher.

Immature Sharp-shinned Hawk in a classic soaring profile (*left*). Note that the tail, when even partially fanned, appears straight cut at the tip — a characteristic of this species. Cape May, October.

Immature Sharp-shinned Hawk, showing the dirty chest (*right*). Cape May, October.

Immature Sharp-shinned Hawk in a glide. Cape May, October.

Immature Cooper's Hawk, showing the classic, long-winged appearance (*top left*). Note the straight cut of the wings along the leading edge. Cape May, October.

Cooper's Hawk in direct flight (*top right*). A notch in the tip of the tail sometimes occurs in this species. Cape May, October.

Immature Cooper's Hawk, illustrating the bull-headed appearance of the species (*bottom left*). Cape May, October.

Immature Cooper's Hawk, soaring (*bottom right*). This individual has the clean white underparts and the dark hangman's hood. Cape May, October.

Adult Cooper's Hawk in a full soar. Adults have stockier proportions overall. Cape May, April.

A pair of immature Cooper's Hawks. Cape May, October.

Immature Cooper's Hawk (*left*) and immature Sharp-shinned Hawk (*right*).
Cape May, October.

Immature Northern Goshawk, showing classic pattern and shape (*top*). Note particularly the heavy spotting on the breast, which mimics a checkerboard pattern. At a distance, the chest looks dirty. Raccoon Ridge, New Jersey, November. Photo by Harry Darrow.

Immature Northern Goshawk, showing wide, tapered wings and long, broad tail that looks more like an extension of the body (*bottom*). Raccoon Ridge, New Jersey, November. Photo by Harry Darrow.

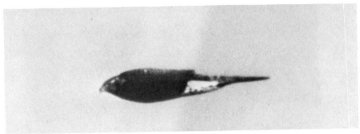

Adult Goshawk in powered flight (*top*). Note the falconlike quality of the wing shape. Raccoon Ridge, New Jersey, November. Photo by Harry Darrow.

Immature Goshawk gliding wing-on (*middle*). Note the heavy body and broad head. Duluth, Minnesota, November.

Adult Goshawk in a soar (*bottom*). The bird shows distinct buteo sympathies. Duluth, Minnesota, November.

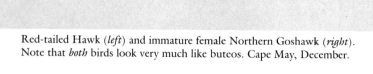

Red-tailed Hawk (*left*) and immature female Northern Goshawk (*right*).
Note that *both* birds look very much like buteos. Cape May, December.

Adult male American Kestrel, hovering. Brigantine National Wildlife Refuge, New Jersey, March.

Female American Kestrel in a glide (*top left*). Cape May, September.

Female American Kestrel, showing the soft angles of the wing (*bottom left*). Lake Henshaw, California, January.

Adult male American Kestrel in a full soar (*right*). Note the translucent "lights" on the trailing edge of the wing. Cape May, October.

Dorsal view of an adult male Merlin. Raccoon Ridge, New Jersey, October.
Photo by Frank Schleicher.

Merlin in a soar, feeding on the wing (*top left*). Cape May, September.

Immature Merlin in a shallow glide (*top right*). Cape May, September.

Immature Merlin, stooping (*bottom left*). Cape May, September.

Merlin, banking sharply (*bottom right*). Note the checkerboard pattern under the wings, which are short and broad. Fire Island, New York, September. Photo by Harry Darrow.

Merlin, giving the impression of overall darkness. Fire Island, New York, September. Photo by Harry Darrow.

Immature Peregrine. Bermuda, October. Photo by Frank Schleicher.

Adult Peregrine (*opposite page*). Forsythe National Wildlife Refuge, New Jersey. Photo by Alan Brady.

Immature Peregrine Falcon in a full soar (*left*). Note the characteristic crossbow shape and the way in which the fanned tail masks the bird's legendary long-winged appearance. Cape May, October.

Adult Peregrine Falcon in a half soar (*center*). Note the very long-tailed appearance and the straight-cut trailing edge on the wing. Cape May, October.

Immature Peregrine Falcon in a shallow glide — the typical Peregrine profile (*right*). Cape May, October.

Adult Peregrine Falcon angling away, showing the upward tilt of the wing (*left*). Cape May, October.

Gliding Peregrine Falcon, angling away (*center*). Cape May, October.

Adult Peregrine Falcon in a tucked-wing glide (*right*). Cape May, October.

Adult Peregrine in powered flight (*top left*). Cape May, New Jersey, October.

Immature, tundra (pale crown) Peregrine in a half-hearted soar (*top right*). Cape May, New Jersey, October.

Adult Prairie Falcon in a soar (*bottom left*). The wings have a less overt taper than a Peregrine's, but the bird still looks very long-winged. San Jacinto, California, January.

Adult Prairie Falcon, showing pale and largish head and rounded hands (a feature that is slightly exaggerated by this photo, *bottom right*). San Jacinto, California, January.

Perched immature *tundrius* Peregrine Falcon (*left*). Note the pale crown; overall, the color is dark. Cape May, September.

Perched adult Prairie Falcon (*right*). In comparison with the bird in photo to left, this falcon appears pale. San Jacinto, California, January.

Immature Prairie Falcon in direct flight. Compare this bird with the Peregrine San Jacinto, California, January.

Immature Peregrine Falcon in direct flight. Cape May, August. Photo by Pete Dunne.

Adult female Gyrfalcon, dark phase, carrying prey. Note the broad overall proportions of the bird and particularly the breadth of the wings and tail. Lancaster, Pennsylvania, March. Photo by Alan Brady.

Adult female Gyrfalcon, dark phase, in direct flight (*opposite page*). Photo by Alan Brady.

Somewhat pale Gyrfalcon, gray phase (*top*). Brigantine National Wildlife Refuge, New Jersey, March. Photo by Jimmy Watson.

Adult male Gyrfalcon, light phase (*above*), and adult female Gyrfalcon, dark phase (*below*). Males and females of this species normally differ in size as shown here (*bottom left*). Lancaster, Pennsylvania, January. Photo by Alan Brady.

Gyrfalcon riding an updraft off a cliff face (*bottom right*). Note the broad, rounded wings, heavy body, and wide tail. These features in combination make the bird greatly resemble a Goshawk. Lancaster, Pennsylvania, March.

Adult male Gyrfalcon, white phase, showing the rounded wing tips and the translucent flight feathers (*opposite page*). Lancaster, Pennsylvania, March. Photo by Alan Brady.

Subadult Mississippi Kite, showing banded tail, mottled underwings, and gray breast. Cape May, June.

Subadult Mississippi Kite in a full soar (*top left*). Note the outward flaring of the tail and its pale windows. Cape May, May.

Adult Mississippi Kite. Note the white-headed but overall dark appearance, the short anterior flight feathers (*top center*), and the flared tail (*top right*) when the bird is in a full soar. Santee River, South Carolina, May.

Mississippi Kite in a typical kite posture (*bottom left*). Note that, except for the large hands, in shape the bird is not unlike a Peregrine Falcon. Santee River, South Carolina, May.

Adult Mississippi Kite, dorsal view, showing the very prominent upperwing patches (*bottom right*). Santee River, South Carolina, May.

American Swallow-tailed Kite. Santee River, South Carolina, May.

American Swallow-tailed Kite in a glide. Note the gull-like droop to the wings. Santee River, South Carolina, May.

American Swallow-tailed Kite in a full soar, showing a fully spread tail and extended primaries. Everglades National Park, Florida, May.

Dorsal view of an American Swallow-tailed Kite in a full soar. Santee River, South Carolina, April.

Black-shouldered Kite, showing the diagnostic dihedral (usually even more pronounced than it appears here, *top left*). Sulphur Springs Valley, Arizona, February.

Immature Black-shouldered Kite, dorsal view (*top right*). Note the darker cast of the back and the smudgy tip on the tail. Sulphur Springs Valley, Arizona, February.

Adult Black-shouldered Kite in a full soar, dorsal view (*bottom left*). Santa Ana National Wildlife Refuge, Texas, March.

Ventral view of a Black-shouldered Kite in a full soar (*bottom right*). This flight posture is less characteristic than gliding or hovering. Santa Barbara, California, February.

Immature Black-shouldered Kite in direct flight. Santa Barbara, California, January.

Immature Northern Harrier in hunting flight. Hackensack Meadows, New Jersey, December. Photo by Frank Schleicher.

Adult male Northern Harrier in a full soar (*opposite page*). Hackensack Meadows, New Jersey, January. Photo by Frank Schleicher.

Immature Northern Harrier. Hackensack Meadows, New Jersey, January.
Photo by Frank Schleicher.

Adult male Northern Harrier, with wings thrown forward in a full soar (*top left*). Ocracoke Island, North Carolina, May.

Immature Northern Harrier, probably male (*top right*). Cape May, October.

Immature Northern Harrier in a glide, showing the falconlike cut of the wings (*bottom left*). Cape May, September.

Adult female Northern Harrier (*bottom right*). Note the very broad wings, characteristic of females of this species.

Adult Turkey Vulture showing the long-tailed silhouette, from which the head is absent, and the deep dihedral. Cape May, October.

Turkey Vulture. Cape May, May.

Kettle of Turkey Vultures. Cape May, November.

Subadult Turkey Vultures with black-tipped yellow bills (*opposite page, top*). The flight feathers shine in the light. Cape May, November.

Turkey Vulture, dorsal view (*opposite page, bottom*). Note that the pale feather shafts in the outer primaries are not usually visible except at very close range. Florida, May.

Silhouettes of a Black Vulture (*left*) and a Turkey Vulture (*right*). Both birds are in a glide posture in the same attitude and at the same altitude. Gettysburg, Pennsylvania, December.

Black Vulture in a classic soaring profile. Cape May, April.

Black Vulture, soaring. Note the flat-winged profile. Florida Prairie, April.

Black Vulture. Florida Prairie, April.

Crested Caracara, a nonmigratory species with a range limited to Florida, southern Texas, and Arizona. Compare this bird with the Black Vulture and the immature Golden Eagle. Florida Prairie, April.

Adult Bald Eagle in a full soar. Bombay Hook, Delaware, August.

Immature Bald Eagle, probably a one-year-old bird. Note that the head and tail are relatively similar in length. Cape May, June.

Adult Bald Eagle, tucked in, riding the updraft off a ridge (*opposite page, top left*). Squaw Creek National Wildlife Refuge, Missouri, January.

Adult Bald Eagle in a glide (*opposite page, top right*). Squaw Creek National Wildlife Refuge, Missouri, February.

Immature Bald Eagle, probably a bird from the most recent breeding season, in a soar (*opposite page, bottom left*). Note the slight downward droop of the wings. Newburyport, Massachusetts, February.

Immature Bald Eagle in very typical plumage (*opposite page, bottom right*).

Immature Bald Eagle, a somewhat stocky and rotund individual (*above*). Cape May, November.

Immature Bald Eagle with a white belly, probably a two-year-old (*opposite page, top*). Squaw Creek National Wildlife Refuge, Missouri, January.

Two immature Bald Eagles in a shallow glide, illustrating the normal range of plumage variation (*opposite page, bottom*). Squaw Creek National Wildlife Refuge, Missouri, January.

Immature Bald Eagles in full soar. Photo by Frank Schleicher.

Subadult Golden Eagle (*opposite page, top*). Note the vestige of white at the base of the flight feathers and the relative length of the head and tail. Cape May, October.

Subadult Golden Eagle in a glide (*opposite page, bottom*).

Female Osprey, wearing a necklace. Cape May, October.

Classic immature Golden Eagle, showing large white wing patches and ringed tail (*opposite page, top left*). Dividing Creek, New Jersey, January.

Immature Golden Eagle in a glide, showing more restricted white patches in the wing than are evident in the previous photo (*opposite page, bottom left*). Cape May, November.

Immature Golden Eagle, showing a good dihedral (*opposite page, right*). Big Bend, Texas, April.

Male Osprey, without a necklace (*left*). North Inlet, South Carolina, September.

Female Osprey in a full soar (*right*). Cape May, October.

Adult female Osprey. Santee River, South Carolina, May.

Osprey with its wings deeply crooked in a set glide. Cape May, October.

Osprey in a glide (*opposite page*). Raccoon Ridge, New Jersey, October. Photo by Frank Schleicher.

Bibliography

American Birds. Seasonal Reports, 1966–1985.

Beebe, Frank L. *Field Studies of the Falconiformes of British Columbia.* British Columbia Provincial Museum, 1974.

Bent, Arthur Cleveland. *Life Histories of North American Birds of Prey.* Vols. 1 and 2. New York: Dover, 1961.

Brett, James, and Alex Nagy. *Feathers in the Wind.* Hawk Mountain Sanctuary Association, 1973.

Broun, Maurice. *Hawks Aloft.* Kutztown, Pa.: Kutztown Publishing, 1948.

Brown, Leslie. *Birds of Prey: Their Biology and Ecology.* New York: A & W Publishers, 1977.

Brown, Leslie, and Dean Amadon. *Eagles, Hawks, and Falcons of the World.* New York: McGraw-Hill, 1968.

Cade, Tom J. *The Falcons of the World.* London: William Collins, 1982.

Clark, William S. "Field Identification of Accipiters in North America." *Birding,* vol. 16, no. 6 (December 1984), 251–263.

Clark, William S., and Michael E. Pramstaller. *Field Identification Pamphlet for North American Raptors.* Raptor Information Center, Washington, D. C.: National Wildlife Federation, 1980.

Dunne, Pete. "How to Tell a Hawk from a Gull: The Road That Led from the Shotgun to the Subjective." *Newsletter of the Hawk Migration Association of North America,* vol. 10, no. 1 (February 1985), 8–10.

Dunne, Pete, Debbie Keller, and Rene Kochenberger. *Hawk Watch: A Guide for Beginners.* Cape May: New Jersey Audubon Society, 1984.

Dunne, Pete, David Sibley, Clay Sutton, and Fred Hamer. "Field Identification of Broad-winged and Red-shouldered Hawk." *Newsletter of the Hawk Migration Association of North America,* vol. 7, no. 1 (February 1982), 8–9.

———. "Flight Identification of Falcons: Wing on at the Limit of Conjecture." *Newsletter of the Hawk Migration Association of North America,* vol. 7, no. 2 (August 1982), 9–10.

———. "The Falcon That Isn't: The Mississippi Kite." *Newsletter of the Hawk Migration Association of North America,* vol. 8, no. 1 (February 1983), 22–24.

Dunne, Pete, and Clay Sutton. "Population Trends in Coastal Raptor Migrants over Ten Years of Cape May Point Autumn Counts." *Records of New Jersey Birds*, vol. 12, no. 3 (Autumn 1986), 39–43.

Habitat Management Series for Unique or Endangered Species. Bureau of Land Management Technical Notes. Washington, D.C.: U.S. Department of the Interior, 1973–1975. [Osprey, Bald Eagle, Northern Goshawk, Ferruginous Hawk, Rough-legged Hawk, Golden Eagle, Merlin, Peregrine Falcon, Prairie Falcon]

Harwood, Michael, ed. *Proceedings of the Hawk Migration Conference, IV*. Rochester, N.Y.: Hawk Migration Association of North America, 1983.

Heintzelman, Donald S. *Autumn Hawk Flights: The Migrations in Eastern North America*. New Brunswick, N.J.: Rutgers University Press, 1975.

———. *A Guide to Hawk Watching in North America*. University Park: Pennsylvania State University Press, 1979.

Journal of the Hawk Migration Association of North America, vol. 2, no. 1 (December 1980).

Julian, Paul R. "Harlan's Hawk: A Challenging Taxonomic and Field Problem." *Colorado Field Ornithology*, no. 1 (Winter 1967), 1–6.

Langley, Lynn. "Swallowtails of the Francis Marion." *South Carolina Wildlife*, vol. 31, no. 5 (September–October 1984), 6–10.

Lish, James W., and William G. Voelker. "Field Identification Aspects of Some Red-tailed Hawk Subspecies." *American Birds*, vol. 40, no. 2 (Summer 1986), 197–202.

Mindell, David P. "Plumage Variation and Winter Range of Harlan's Hawk." *American Birds*, vol. 39, no. 2 (Summer 1985), 127–133.

Mueller, Helmut C., Daniel D. Berger, and George Allez. "The Identification of North American Accipiters." *American Birds*, vol. 33, no. 3 (May 1979), 236–240.

Newsletter of the Hawk Migration Association of North America. Seasonal Reports, 1977–1985.

Newton, Ian. *Population Ecology of Raptors*. Vermillion, S.Dak.: Buteo Books, 1979.

Peterson, Roger Tory. *A Field Guide to the Birds of Eastern and Central North America*. 4th ed. Boston: Houghton Mifflin, 1980.

Porter, R. F., Ian Willis, Steen Christensen, and Bent Pors Nielsen. *Flight Identification of European Raptors*. Calton, England: T. and A. D. Poyser, 1981.

Ratcliffe, Derek. *The Peregrine Falcon*. Vermillion, S.Dak.: Buteo Books, 1980.

Robbins, Chandler S., Bertel Bruun, and Herbert S. Zim. *Birds of North America*. New York: Golden Press, 1966.

Scott, Shirley L., ed. *Field Guide to the Birds of North America*. Washington, D.C.: National Geographic Society, 1983.

"Sticky Problems of Hawk Identification." Panel discussion. In *Proceedings of the Hawk Migration Conference, IV*. Syracuse, N.Y.: Hawk Migration Association of North America, 1974.

Sutton, Clay C., and Patricia Taylor Sutton. "The Spring Hawk Migration at Cape May, New Jersey." *Cassinia*, no. 60 (1983), 5–18.

Watson, Donald. *The Hen Harrier*. Berkhamsted, Hertfordshire: T. and A. D. Poyser, 1977.

White, Clayton M., and Tom J. Cade. "Cliff Nesting Raptors and Ravens along the Colville River in Arctic Alaska." In *The Living Bird*. Ithaca, N.Y.: Cornell Laboratory of Ornithology, 1971.

Index